JOURNEY THROUGH THE BIBLE

KEN WADE

Other books by Ken Wade

Del Delker
Jesus for a New Millennium
Journey Through the Bible: From Genesis to Job
Journey to Moriah
The Orion Conspiracy
Paul: A Spiritual Journey

By Don Schneider with Ken Wade

Really Living
Really Living 2

By Jon Osborne with Ken Wade

Back on Track

JOURNEY THROUGH THE BIBLE

KEN WADE

The Voice of Prophecy

FROM PSALMS TO MALACHI

Pacific Press®
Publishing Association

Nampa, Idaho | Oshawa, Ontario, Canada
www.pacificpress.com

Cover design by Gerald Lee Monks
Cover design resources from iStockphoto.com
Inside design by Kristin Hansen-Mellish

The author assumes full responsibility for the accuracy of all facts and quotations as cited in this book.

Additional copies of this book may be obtained by calling toll-free 1-800-765-6955 or online at www.adventistbookcenter.com.

Library of Congress Cataloging-in-Publication Data:

Wade, Kenneth R., 1951–
Journey through the Bible from Psalms to Malachi / Ken Wade.
    p. cm.
  ISBN 13: 978-0-8163-4433-8 (pbk.)
  ISBN 10: 0-8163-4433-7 (pbk.)
  1. Bible. O.T.—Commentaries. I. Title.
BS1151.52.W332 2013
221.7—dc23
                              2012051228

13 14 15 16 17 • 5 4 3 2 1

Contents

Preface

When at the beginning of the year 2000 our Voice of Prophecy staff decided to begin a journey through the entire Bible, preparing radio broadcasts focusing on each book individually, I had no idea what a great adventure we had embarked upon.

Our journey through the Bible, along with other programs focusing specifically on the Gospels, filled most of the next three years of my life. It gave me the opportunity to study the Book of books in greater depth than I ever had before.

There had been times during my ministry when I had challenged myself to read the Bible through in a year. One year I actually made it through by the middle of May; most years, I got bogged down and never finished.

Now I assigned myself to read each book of the Bible not once or twice but three or more times. With each book, I strove to grasp its central message and find a way to present that message to the listening public in ten to twelve minutes—in a way that would interest them instead of making them want to tune to another station.

This book, and the preceding and following volumes, are the product of our Voice of Prophecy journey through the Bible, with many additions that have been made in the ten years since we first completed the journey series.

If you're ready to take the journey through the Book of books from cover to cover, I trust that the material we developed at the Voice of Prophecy will help you to grasp the central message of each book, and perhaps encourage you to persevere through some of the portions that may have seemed obscure or difficult to you in the past. Join me on the journey. I'm sure you won't regret it!

Ken Wade
Fall 2012

CHAPTER 1

Psalms: God's Hymnbook

There's an old story that's based on a passage from the Psalms. It's a wonderful report of how God answered the prayers of a group of Christians many years ago in an amazing way, just as they asked. Now, when you read the story, it's just possible that you may react in the way I've sometimes heard people in difficult situations respond to miracle stories. In fact, I've sometimes had this kind of reaction myself when something I've prayed for hasn't received a positive answer.

I've prayed for the healing of friends and great servants of the Lord, expecting that if anyone ought to receive the benefit of one of God's miracles, surely this person was a prime candidate.

But no miracle occurred.

So I can understand why some people say, "You know, Pastor, I don't really want to hear that story. I've heard people tell all kinds of miracle stories. But where's *my* miracle? God doesn't answer my prayers that way! Why don't you tell me some stories about *un*answered prayers? Or about prayers to which God answered No!

A MIRACLE IS A MIRACLE, BY DEFINITION, *BECAUSE* IT IS AN UNUSUAL HAPPENING.

That's where I am right now. I'm not getting any positive answers."

If that's where you are today, I can relate. I've been there myself.

And I want to assure you that I understand. There's something that a lot of people don't take into consideration when it comes to miracles. There are preachers who promise miracles to everyone. But they apparently never stop to think about something very important: a miracle is a miracle, by definition, *because* it is an unusual happening. It's out of the ordinary. It's not something we should expect every day.

Consider this: if someone promises you that God will always work a miracle in your behalf, that person probably doesn't even understand what a miracle is! Yes, it's OK to pray for miracles. But if someone is telling you that you can *expect* a miracle? That's different.

So, if you've been wondering why God doesn't grant you miracles every time you pray, I want to assure you that the biblical book of Psalms was written by people who not only prayed for miracles but also waited through long, dark nights of the soul, wondering when God would come to their aid.

We'll unpack that a bit in a moment, but before then, let me share a story of answered prayer with you. A story like this encourages me to keep on praying, and I hope it'll do the same for you.

It happened back in the 1920s, shortly after the founding of the school that's now known as Dallas Theological Seminary. The school had fallen on financial hard times—in fact, they were almost bankrupt. Things

> A STORY LIKE THIS ENCOURAGES ME TO KEEP ON PRAYING.

went from bad to worse until the day when the creditors announced that they were ready to foreclose on their loans and close down the school. If the problems weren't resolved by noon that day, the school would be history.

That very morning the school's president, Dr. Lewis Sperry Chafer, called a group of people together in his office for prayer. One of the men who was there was Harry Ironside. When it was Harry's turn to pray, he said something like this: "Lord, we know that the cattle on a thousand hills are Thine. Please sell some of them and send us the money." His prayer was based on the Lord's words as expressed in Psalm 50:10: "Every beast of the forest is Mine, and the cattle on a thousand hills" (NKJV).

Now, this seems hard to believe, but it really happened this way: While those people were praying in the president's office, a tall Texan with boots on and an open collar walked into the school's business office and said, "I just sold two carloads of cattle in Fort Worth. I've been trying to make a business deal, but it fell through, and I feel compelled to give the money to the seminary. I don't know if you need it or not, but here's the check!"

A secretary took the check and, knowing how critical things were financially, went to the door of the office where the group was praying and timidly tapped. When she finally got a response, Dr. Chafer took one look at the check and realized that it was for exactly the amount needed to forestall the foreclosure!

Then he noticed that the check had been made out by a well-known cattleman in payment for—well, you know what. He turned and looked at Dr. Ironside and said, "Well, Harry, it looks like God answered your prayer. He sold the cattle!"[1]

I love stories like that, don't you? They remind me that we do have a God in heaven who loves to answer our prayers.

But stories like that can be troubling too. They can leave us with some pretty difficult, unanswered questions, like this one asked in Psalm 13:

> How long, O LORD? Will you forget me forever?
>   How long will you hide your face from me?
> How long must I wrestle with my thoughts
>   and every day have sorrow in my heart?
>   How long will my enemy triumph over me?
> Look on me and answer, O LORD my God.
>   Give light to my eyes, or I will sleep in death
>   (verses 1–3, NIV).

This is a psalm of King David, who certainly experienced his share of trials—as well as triumphs—in his life. He must have written this poem during a very bleak time when he was still waiting to see answers to his prayers.

PERHAPS YOU CAN RESONATE WITH THE PLIGHT OF THE DEAR OLD GRANDMOTHER.

Some time ago here at Voice of Prophecy we received a letter from India. Perhaps you can resonate with the plight of the dear old grandmother whose situation was described in the letter.

She's a widow, and so are her two daughters. (The story kind of reminds you of the story of Naomi and Ruth, doesn't it? But these women's situation is even worse.)

These three widows live in two little mud huts in a village in India, and they are struggling to support eight children! But there are no nearby fields of barley that they can glean in, and no rich uncle to woo in hopes of redemption. The only employment these women can get is hand-rolling cigarettes at a local factory.

For a day's work, they are paid about ninety cents. But the work is destroying their health. Just imagine what the nicotine in the tobacco is doing to them as they roll it with bare hands all day long!

Dorothy Eaton Watts told us about the plight of this grandmother and also told us what the old woman said when Dorothy shared some Bible promises about God's blessings with her. The poor, sick old grandmother looked up at her and said, "Yes, God *can* do anything, but to us He has *not* been merciful! I pray that God would let me die soon, for I cannot bear to see the misery of my children!"

Do you hear an echo of Psalm 13 in that story? Do you ever cry out with the psalmist, "Look on me and answer, O LORD my God. Give light to my eyes, or I will sleep in death"?

How do you keep on going in life when everything is going wrong and God doesn't seem to be hearing your prayers anymore?

When you find yourself feeling that way, you're not alone. In fact, you're in the company of many people whose thoughts and prayers have been recorded in the Bible, in the book of Psalms.

We call the book of Psalms God's hymnbook, because it's made up of poems that were originally set to music. But, even though the psalms were written by many different people under many different circumstances, the Lord has seen fit to include this collection of poetry in our Bible. It's just as much a part of God's inspired Word as any other part.

And really, it's a great book because of the way it gets down in the trenches and struggles with some of the hard questions of life. When things are going badly in life, you

GOD ACCEPTS YOUR FEELINGS, JUST AS HE ACCEPTS THE WORDS OF THE PSALMIST.

can find a psalm that resonates with your feelings—and in it you'll discover that God doesn't get angry with you for expressing your disappointment or frustration to Him. He accepts your feelings, just as He accepts the words of the psalmist.

All of us have heard the words of Psalm 23, the shepherd's psalm, written by King David. Maybe you've even memorized it. I can still recite it from the King James Version, which I memorized as a boy.

14

The Lord is my shepherd; I shall not want. He maketh me to lie down in green pastures: he leadeth me beside the still waters. . . . Surely goodness and mercy shall follow me all the days of my life: and I will dwell in the house of the Lord for ever (verses 1, 2, 6).

It's a wonderful, positive psalm, full of assurance that even when we walk through the valley of the shadow of death, God will be there to comfort us and protect us and prepare good food for us to eat, even as our enemies prowl about the perimeter, looking for a way to defeat us!

DAVID COULD WRITE THE SHEPHERD'S PSALM, BUT HE COULD ALSO EXPRESS DESPAIR TO THE LORD.

But how often do we hear the words of the immediately adjacent Psalm 22 repeated—other than the first few words, which Jesus quoted while He was dying on the cross? This psalm was also written by David, and it begins like this:

My God, My God, why have You forsaken Me?
Why are You so far from helping Me,
And from the words of My groaning?
O My God, I cry in the daytime, but You do not hear;
And in the night season, and am not silent.

David continues questioning God by reminding Him that in the past He delivered His people from their troubles, but that He's not doing anything for David right now:

Our fathers trusted in You;
They trusted, and You delivered them.
They cried to You, and were delivered;
They trusted in You, and were not ashamed.
But I am a worm, and no man;
A reproach of men, and despised by the people
(verses 1, 2, 4–6, NKJV).

When you read that psalm, it can help you realize that you're not alone in your struggles. David could write the shepherd's psalm, but he could also express despair to the Lord.

The book of Psalms is a book we can turn to in times of great joy, and in times of great need.

But as you turn to the psalms in times of crisis or disappointment, notice something important about them. Notice, for instance, how Psalm 13 ends. Remember, this is the psalm that begins with the words, "How long, O Lord? Will you forget me forever? How long will You hide Your face from me?" (NKJV).

The psalm ends on a more positive note, with these words:

> I have trusted in Your mercy;
> My heart shall rejoice in Your salvation.
> I will sing to the Lord,
> Because He has dealt bountifully with me
> (verses 5, 6, NKJV).

Even in this psalm, with the "unlucky" number 13, where the psalmist is crying out that nothing is going right, he still looks for and finds evidences of God's mercy.

And in the midst of Psalm 22, we find these words:

> You have answered Me.
> I will declare Your name to My brethren;
> In the midst of the assembly I will praise You
> (verses 21, 22, NKJV).

Psalm 30:5 reminds us that "weeping may endure for a night, but joy comes in the morning" (NKJV).

And with that thought in mind, let me share a bit more of the story of the three widows in India. Their huts were located in a squatter community on public land.

THE WOMEN PRAISE THE LORD FOR THAT LITTLE RAY OF SUNSHINE.

There came a day when the local officials decided to deal with the squatter problem, and they demolished most of the huts. But when they saw the conditions of the three widows, they left their huts there and actually deeded the land to them so they wouldn't have to move.

A small blessing, perhaps, in an otherwise dreary, depressing existence, but the women praise the Lord for that little ray of sunshine.

Whatever your circumstances, whatever your need, there is a poem in God's magnificent hymnbook to match your mood. If it's a great day of joy for you, turn to the end of the book—the last six psalms are all songs of praise. So are the psalms around Psalm 100.

If you're feeling bad about something you've done, read Psalm 51, David's great psalm of repentance.

And for everyday life, how can you beat that all-time favorite, Psalm 23, the shepherd's psalm?

In whatever circumstances life finds us, we can still know that the Lord is our Shepherd—and even when we do experience want or walk through the valley of the shadow of death, He has not abandoned us. Even when we cry out in our despair, waiting for some sign that He hears us, we can rest assured that He does. And that He has a good plan for our lives.

Especially for our eternal life.

What a joy it will be to dwell "in the house of the Lord forever."

Ah, the psalms. They can lift us to the heights, but they will also walk with us through the depths of life. Take them, read them, sing them if you can. And walk with the Lord—through all the high and low places of your life.

ENDNOTE

1. James S. Hewett, *Illustrations Unlimited* (Wheaton, IL: Tyndale, 1988), 419. Name of the original president of the seminary located at http://www.dts.edu/about/history/.

CHAPTER 2

Proverbs: Wisdom for Today

How should we read the book of Proverbs? How should we react to its wisdom?

Is it an up-to-date advice column that we should turn to whenever we need to make a decision? Or is it perhaps a little bit old-fashioned and *passé*—just something to read to see how people thought about things three thousand years ago?

> THE BOOK DOESN'T SET ITSELF UP AS THAT TYPE OF FINAL-ANSWER BOOK.

Proverbs is in the Bible, so does that mean we should treat it as God's final word on whatever topics it addresses?

Or is it, perhaps, just a series of observations about what works and doesn't work in life?

I want to take a look at a number of the proverbs found in this book and use them to illustrate what I think is the best way to read the book.

Would it shock you if I were to tell you that I don't think we should take Proverbs as God's final word of wisdom about everything in life?

Would I really dare say that?

Yes.

Why?

Well, for one thing, the book doesn't set itself up as that type of final-answer book. Rather, it is a book

for learning what wisdom and discipline are,

> for understanding words of deep meaning,
> for acquiring an enlightened attitude of mind
>   —virtue, justice and fair-dealing;
> for teaching sound judgment to the ignorant,
>   and knowledge and sense to the young
>   (Proverbs 1:2–4, *Jerusalem Bible*).

It presents itself as a book of sound parental advice: "Listen, my son, to your father's instruction, do not reject your mother's teaching" (verse 8, *Jerusalem Bible*).

While we tend to think of it as a book written entirely by Solomon, it actually contains several sections. Chapters 1–9 are an introduction in which a father gives advice to his son about how to live wisely. The next twelve chapters are given the heading "The Proverbs of Solomon," and then in the middle of chapter 22, we find the heading "Sayings of the Sages." Chapter 25 begins another series of proverbs of Solomon with some additional material "from the sages."

The last two chapters of the book include "The Sayings of Agur," and "The Sayings of Lemuel."

All these wise sayings were collected together at some point and made into a book that forms part of our Bible. But does that mean that because it is part of God's Holy Book, it is the be-all and end-all of wisdom?

There's something interesting you'll notice if you read the book carefully. Let me illustrate it this way:

Years ago, I remember seeing a little bear-shaped bottle of honey with a Bible text printed on the label. "My child, eat honey, for it is good, and the drippings of the honeycomb are sweet to your taste" (Proverbs 24:13, NRSV).

Now, if you take it seriously, it almost seems as though the Bible is commanding you to eat honey!

IF YOU TAKE IT SERIOUSLY, IT ALMOST SEEMS AS THOUGH THE BIBLE IS COMMANDING YOU TO EAT HONEY!

But here's something curious: the company that labeled that honey bottle could have chosen to put this text on the label instead: "If you have found honey, eat only enough for you, or else, having too much, you will vomit it" (Proverbs 25:16, NRSV).

Or, why didn't they use this text? "It is not good to eat much honey, or to seek honor on top of honor" (verse 27, NRSV).

It doesn't take a PhD in sales and marketing to understand why the honey manufacturer would choose one text above another to place on its label. But all of these texts are in the Bible—in the book of Proverbs. So aren't they all equally worthy of being placed on a honey bottle?

Well, this is a bit of a light-hearted example. But I think if we look at it closely, we may learn something that's important for us to put into practice as we read and apply the Bible to daily life.

Are you ever tempted—I have to admit that I am—to look for a Bible text to support your point of view?

After all, if I can find a text that says something like what I want to persuade people of, then that should be the final word, shouldn't it? You can't argue with a Bible text!

But is that really the way we should use the Bible? Is that really the way we should study the Bible—just looking for texts that support our viewpoints?

Do you think that was God's intention in giving us His Word? Do you think He wants us constantly dragging Him into the battle on our side?

If you do, please get ahold of volume 1 in this series and read the chapter on the book of 1 Samuel, or go to the Voice of Prophecy Web site (www.vop.com) and listen to the program on 1 Samuel. (You can find it in the program archives for the year 2012.) When we dealt with that book, we discussed the story about the time the Israelites took the ark of the covenant into battle with them.

That story, along with Proverbs, teaches an important principle: When you read the Bible, let it speak for itself. Don't try to drag God into the battle on your side. Don't go looking for the parts that agree with your viewpoint. You might miss the most important parts—the parts that might help to change your thinking to be more like God's!

DON'T INSIST THAT GOD THINK LIKE YOU.

Don't insist that God think like you. Let God speak to you through the Bible.

Another thing that you'll notice as you read through Proverbs is that it sometimes seems to come down on both sides of a question. Not that it contradicts itself, but that the advice it gives is ultimately very practical—dare we say pragmatic?

Consider, for instance, two proverbs about the usefulness of wealth:

> The wealth of the rich is their fortress;
>> the poverty of the poor is their ruin
>> (Proverbs 10:15, NRSV).

> Those who trust in their riches will wither,
>> but the righteous will flourish like green leaves
>> (Proverbs 11:28, NRSV).

WE MUST BE CAREFUL NOT TO TAKE ITS OBSERVATIONS AS PRESCRIPTIONS.

The first proverb looks at one aspect of the value of wealth: it can be a protection in times of trouble—like a fortress that people can run to. But the second proverb looks at wealth from the opposite angle and discourages people from trusting in their wealth for protection. These verses don't contradict each other, but they illustrate an important point about the intent of the Proverbs.

This is a book of practical wisdom. Some of it is what you could call *observational wisdom.* Kind of a "what I've learned about life by observing" book.

Other parts are more prescriptive. Advising what one *should* do.

But it's important not to confuse the two types of wisdom.

Consider the following texts for example. Would you say they are observational or prescriptive?

> A bribe is like a magic stone in the eyes of those who give it;
>> wherever they turn they prosper (Proverbs 17:8, NRSV).

> A gift in secret averts anger;
>> and a concealed bribe in the bosom, strong wrath
>> (Proverbs 21:14, NRSV).

Is the Bible prescribing bribery as a way to get ahead in life? If you think so, you also need to read Proverbs 17:23.

> The wicked accept a concealed bribe
>> to pervert the ways of justice (NRSV).

No way is the Bible prescribing that we be wicked and accept bribes; but in the book of Proverbs, we do find many verses that are simply observations about the way life actually works. It's a very practical book in that way, but we must be careful not to take its observations as prescriptions. Let's face it. Bribes often work. And Proverbs *observes* that fact without *prescribing* bribery.

It's important to understand the difference between observation and prescription as you read the book of Proverbs. Otherwise it can seem confusing, and maybe even self-contradictory.

Now, on to another question about Proverbs. Is its wisdom outdated? Consider this text for example:

> A whip for the horse, a bridle for the donkey,
>   and a rod for the back of fools (Proverbs 26:3, NRSV).

You probably don't use a whip or a bridle on a daily basis. And I certainly wouldn't advise you to carry a rod around and start beating on anyone that you consider a fool. So, perhaps, this particular proverb doesn't have a lot of practical value to us in the twenty-first century.

Here's another proverb that at first glance might seem a little dated:

> The lazy person says, "There is a lion in the road!
>   There is a lion in the streets!" (verse 13, NRSV).

You probably haven't used the excuse of a lion in the streets on a Monday morning when you just didn't feel like going in to work. But stop and think for a moment. This proverb is intended to discourage people from being lazy and finding any excuse they can to avoid work.

IT DOESN'T MATTER WHETHER YOUR EXCUSE IS TOO MANY LIONS OR TOO MANY JAGUARS IN THE STREET.

It just needs a little updating to be as true as ever. Perhaps today a person would decide not to go to work because "it looks like it's going to snow." Or maybe "the traffic's too bad today."

It doesn't matter whether your excuse is too many lions or too many Jaguars in the street. Proverbs is still calling you out for being lazy!

Now, here's a proverb that's as current as tomorrow's headlines:

The rich rule over the poor,
   and the borrower is the slave of the lender
   (Proverbs 22:7, NRSV).

When Solomon penned these words, he was probably thinking about a person who had gone to a rich man in his village and asked to borrow a little money to tide him over through some lean months. Then when it came time to pay back the debt, the poor fellow didn't have the money to do it, and soon he found himself a servant—working for the rich man to pay back what he had borrowed. Many people in Solomon's day lost their freedom in that very way—becoming servants or slaves because of debt.

> THE PROVERB IS STILL TRUE, AND INDIVIDUALS AS WELL AS GOVERNMENTS NEED TO CONSIDER ITS WISDOM.

Maybe we don't see people becoming slaves in just that way these days. But we do hear a lot about debt.

The world is in the middle of one of the worst debt crises in history. Entire nations teeter on the edge of bankruptcy. Millions of Americans are hanging on by the skin of their teeth, living in houses that are worth less money than they borrowed to purchase them. There is growing anger of the "99 percent" against the "1 percent."

Students are graduating from college with loans it will take them until retirement to pay off.

And there are no easy solutions. Once you're in debt, you're obligated to pay.

You may not become a literal slave. But if you find yourself working extra shifts, taking on a second job, or visiting the payday advance office every couple weeks, well . . .

The proverb is still true, and individuals as well as governments need to consider its wisdom.

Here's another proverb that's just as up-to-date as the day it was written:

Who has woe?
Who has sorrow?
Who has contentions?
Who has complaints?

Who has wounds without cause?
Who has redness of eyes?
Those who linger long at the wine,
Those who go in search of mixed wine.
Do not look on the wine when it is red,
When it sparkles in the cup,
When it swirls around smoothly;
At the last it bites like a serpent,
And stings like a viper (NKJV).

That counsel is found in Proverbs 23:29–32, and it's just as apropos today as it was three thousand years ago.

Recent research has unveiled the way that alcohol and other addictive drugs work in the brain—and it's a whole lot like the sting of a viper. Dr. Alan Leshner, director of the National Institute on Drug Abuse, puts it this way: " 'Drugs of abuse change the brain, hijack its motivational systems and even change how its genes function.' "[1]

Once an addictive substance gets its teeth into you, its poison circulates through your system, changing everything. Soon, stopping becomes almost impossible. As Dr. Leshner puts it, addiction " 'may start with the voluntary act of taking drugs, but once you've got it, you can't just tell the addict "Stop," any more than you can tell the smoker "Don't have emphysema." ' "[2] Scientists now realize that addiction becomes a physical problem just as much as emphysema or a snakebite is a physical problem.

PROVERBS ILLUSTRATES TO US THE FOLLY OF READING THE BIBLE SELECTIVELY.

All the more reason why that old proverb, "Do not look on the wine when it is red, when it sparkles in the cup," is still good advice today. In fact, the proverb could be expanded to warn us against a lot of temptations that hadn't yet been dreamed up when it was written.

We've examined only a few tiny slices of the wisdom recorded in the biblical book of Proverbs, but its core message is found in two key verses:

"The fear of the LORD is the beginning of wisdom,
And the knowledge of the Holy One is understanding"
(Proverbs 9:10, NKJV).

"Wisdom is the principal thing;
Therefore get wisdom.
And in all your getting, get understanding"
    (Proverbs 4:7, NKJV).

The wisdom and knowledge that is most important to us in life all begins with God, who is the Source of all wisdom. Most of what we read in Proverbs is just plain good old common sense—to a person who knows the Lord.

Knowledge of God and His holiness and knowledge of His Word are step one for learning whatever we may need to know about life.

Putting aside our own supposed wisdom is step two.

And a proper reading of Proverbs instructs us in how best to take that crucial step. What I mean is, Proverbs illustrates to us the folly of reading the Bible selectively—just looking for the texts that support our own viewpoints. We need to read the Bible more carefully, letting God actually speak to us, sharing *His* viewpoint.

When we seek God's wisdom and put aside our own wisdom, we open ourselves up to being led by God's Holy Spirit in the way of God.

So, take the Proverbs, take the entire Bible. Read it regularly. Let the Word of the Lord sink in deep and be the beginning of your wisdom (not just an affirmation of your own way of thinking). Let the Lord lead you in every part of your life. You'll never regret it.

ENDNOTES

1. Sharon Begley, "How It All Starts Inside Your Brain," *Newsweek,* February 12, 2001, 40.

2. Ibid., 42.

CHAPTER 3

Ecclesiastes: The Search for Meaning

In his book *Man's Search for Meaning,* Victor Frankl tells of his life in Nazi concentration camps during World War II. During three long, hard years, he watched hundreds of men give up living— they'd just lie down one day and refuse to get up, no matter how they were threatened or beaten.

But others kept on keeping on—somehow clinging to hope for a better future, hope that they would see their loved ones again, hope that someday their long night of suffering would be over.

By early 1945, the inmates in the camps had some inkling that liberation might come soon. In fact, one of Frankl's fellow prisoners had a dream, and in that dream someone revealed to him exactly when the deliverance would take place.

The man pulled Frankl aside one day and confided his most precious secret: "In my dream," he said, "I was told that we would be liberated on March 30."

> IN THAT DREAM SOMEONE REVEALED TO HIM EXACTLY WHEN THE DELIVERANCE WOULD TAKE PLACE.

With this hope in his heart, Frankl's friend began to go about his daily drudgeries with new enthusiasm, new hope.

But as the month of March began to wane, and there was no sign that Allied troops were getting anywhere near their camp, the man's hope waned as well. Then on March 29, he fell ill. By the next day, he had lost consciousness. He died on March 31.

After telling this story, Frankl—who was a medical doctor and psychiatrist—draws this conclusion:

> Those who know how close the connection is between the state of mind of a man—his courage and hope, or lack of them—and the state of immunity of his body will understand that the sudden loss of hope and courage can have a deadly effect. The ultimate cause of my friend's death was that the expected liberation did not come and he was severely disappointed. This suddenly lowered his body's resistance against the latent typhus infection. His faith in the future and his will to live had become paralyzed and his body fell victim to illness.[1]

WITHOUT HOPE WE HARDLY HAVE THE STRENGTH TO RISE UP EACH MORNING AND FACE THE DAY.

Hope is an extremely important ingredient in our lives. It's like yeast in bread—without it we hardly have the strength to rise up each morning and face the day.

So how do we relate to a book like Ecclesiastes? On a quick reading, the book might seem to you like a prescription for pessimism.

Consider a few choice verses:

> It is useless, useless, said the Philosopher. Life is useless, all useless. You spend your life working, laboring, and what do you have to show for it? Generations come and generations go, but the world stays just the same (Ecclesiastes 1:2–4).

I'm using the *Good News Bible* in this chapter because it puts the Bible's message in language that resonates with how people talk about life today.

If those verses didn't take the wind out of your sails, try this verse: "Everything leads to weariness—a weariness too great for words. Our eyes can never see enough to be satisfied; our ears can never hear enough" (verse 8).

And top that off with this:

> I came to regret that I had worked so hard. You work for

something with all your wisdom, knowledge, and skill, and then you have to leave it all to someone who hasn't had to work for it. It is useless, and it isn't right! (Ecclesiastes 2:20, 21).

Are you discouraged yet? Well, let me add just a couple more verses to illustrate what I mean about Ecclesiastes. On the surface, it appears to be a pure downer—a douser of all the flames of hope that may burn in your heart. But trust me. Stick with me. I won't spend this whole chapter dwelling on the negative verses. But I do want you to be prepared for the type of reading you will encounter when you read the book:

> I realized another thing, that in this world fast runners do not always win the races, and the brave do not always win the battles. The wise do not always earn a living, intelligent people do not always get rich, and capable people do not always rise to high positions. Bad luck happens to everyone. You never know when your time is coming. Like birds suddenly caught in a trap, like fish caught in a net, we are trapped at some evil moment when we least expect it (Ecclesiastes 9:11, 12).

I must confess that these last two verses came to mind when I heard the news recently about a terrible Saturday-night crash on a Florida freeway, in which

THE PASTOR WHO WAS IN A HURRY TO BE AT HIS POST OF DUTY WAS THE ONE WHO SUFFERED.

dozens of cars and trucks smashed into one another in thick smoke and fog.

A pastor and his family were on their way home from a church conference when they found themselves snared in that miasma.

He, his wife, and one of their daughters were all killed in the pileup.

Another pastor from the same church had decided not to hurry back home to Georgia for Sunday morning worship, and because he stayed behind, his life was spared.

It doesn't seem fair, does it, that the pastor who was in a hurry to be at his post of duty was the one who suffered? Perhaps Solomon had seen that sort of thing happen in his own life, and when he penned these verses, he was in a very discouraged state of mind.

But wait. Before you fall into discouragement with him, let me remind and reassure you that we are going to find much that is positive in this biblical book as well.

I shared these verses because they are an important aspect of Ecclesiastes. It does have its negative side. In fact, there is no other book in the Bible that packs such a potent punch of negativity!

> Enjoy life, but don't go over Fool's Hill and stay there.

And you might find yourself asking: Isn't the Bible supposed to be a Book of hope? If so, what is a book like Ecclesiastes doing in it? Does it share even a glimmer of hope?

Well, yes, in fact, it does! There are actually parts of it that echo that good old Bobby McFerrin song, "Don't Worry, Be Happy!"

For example, consider chapter 3, verses 12 and 13: "I realized that all we can do is be happy and do the best we can while we are still alive. All of us should eat and drink and enjoy what we have worked for. It is God's gift."

And how about chapter 8, verse 15: "I am convinced that we should enjoy ourselves, because the only pleasure we have in this life is eating and drinking and enjoying ourselves. We can at least do this as we labor during the life that God has given us in this world."

And Ecclesiastes' advice to the young is, "Young people, enjoy your youth. Be happy while you are still young. Do what you want to do, and follow your heart's desire. But remember that God is going to judge you for whatever you do" (Ecclesiastes 11:9). That's good, practical advice, isn't it? Enjoy life, but don't go over Fool's Hill and stay there. Even on the far side, God will be watching you.

So there are both upbeat and downbeat portions in the book. Things that would discourage you from enjoying life as well as verses that encourage you to be joyful while remaining respectful toward God.

What, exactly, is this book? And what is it doing in the Bible?

King Solomon was probably the author of Ecclesiastes, which is interesting when you consider that some of Ecclesiastes's wisdom seems to run counter to the positive, affirming tone of Proverbs.

Many of the things the author says fit well with Solomon's story. He speaks of himself as a ruler in Jerusalem, and he says that he became greater than all who were in Jerusalem before him. He speaks also of how prosperous he was and how he sought wisdom. He also mentions the large number of slaves, wives, and concubines he had, and the great works that he built—all things that match what we know about Solomon.

He goes on to say that he applied his wisdom to trying to figure out the purpose of life; he basically tried everything he could think of—from involving himself in a workaholic flurry of activity to trying out various types of beverages designed to make him feel happy and erase the pain of his existence.

LIFE DOES MAKE SENSE AFTER ALL, WHEN YOU INCLUDE GOD AND ETERNITY IN THE EQUATION.

But after all of that, he became discouraged with life, questioning whether any of it had meaning; after all, he pointed out, we come into the world naked, and we leave the same way.

And you know, if that was the final conclusion of the book of Ecclesiastes, I guess I'd question whether the book really ought to be a part of a hopeful book such as the Bible.

But that isn't the conclusion. That isn't the way the book ends.

Here are the last two verses of the book:

> After all this, there is only one thing to say: Have reverence for God, and obey his commands, because this is all that man was created for. God is going to judge everything we do, whether good or bad, even things done in secret (Ecclesiastes 12:13, 14).

So, after looking at life and dwelling at length on the discouraging aspects of it—while still trying to encourage people to be happy and enjoy life—Solomon arrives at an important conclusion: *what really matters is our relationship with God.*

That's what keeps life from being a mere meaningless chasing after wind.

Solomon admits that when you look at life from a purely human, temporal point of view, nothing has meaning. But then, at the end of the book, he stops, looks around him again, and takes a heavenward glance. Suddenly everything changes, and he begins to look at life through God's eyes.

Now, in the blink of an eye, his entire outlook changes. He begins to see that life does make sense after all, when you include God and eternity in the equation. When you realize that God intends to weigh all the events of earth in His balances, all of a sudden what we do has meaning!

Because there's more than just this life to consider. There's eternal life—a heaven to win and a hell to shun! That's where everything makes sense in the end, for if we give our lives to God and let Him work His way in us, we have the privilege of living with Him for all eternity—where the things we do last forever and are not just "chasing after wind."

It's God who pulls it all into focus—His love, but also His justice, in assuring us that life has meaning because He has given it meaning.

In his book *Loving God,* Chuck Colson tells a story that brings the message of Ecclesiastes down to our day. It's a story that starts out a lot like Victor Frankl's story that I shared at the beginning of this chapter.

But, like the book of Ecclesiastes, it has a much more upbeat ending. Here's the story, as Colson tells it:

> If we would love God, we must love His justice and act upon it. . . . That was certainly one of Alexander Solzhenitsyn's greatest discoveries in the Soviet gulag.
>
> Like other prisoners, Solzhenitsyn worked in the fields, his days a pattern of backbreaking labor and slow starvation. One day the hopelessness became too much to bear. Solzhenitsyn felt no purpose in fighting on; his life would make no ultimate difference. Laying his shovel down, he walked slowly to a crude work-site bench. He knew at any moment a guard would order him up and, when he failed to respond, bludgeon him to death, probably with his own shovel. He'd seen it happen many times.
>
> As he sat waiting, head down, he felt a presence. Slowly he lifted his eyes. Next to him sat an old man with a wrinkled, utterly expressionless face. Hunched over, the man drew a stick through the sand at Solzhenitsyn's feet, deliberately tracing out the sign of the cross.

IN THE LIGHT OF THE CROSS WE SEE THERE IS SO MUCH MORE.

As Solzhenitsyn stared at that rough outline, his entire perspective shifted. He knew he was merely one man against the all-powerful Soviet empire. Yet in that moment, he also knew that the hope of all mankind was represented by that simple cross—and through its power, anything was possible. Solzhenitsyn slowly got up, picked up his shovel, and went back to work, not knowing that his writings on truth and freedom would one day inflame the whole world.[2]

Life can be discouraging. Sometimes we feel the way Solomon did—that we're just chasing after wind. But in the light of the Cross we see there is so much more. Because God has been willing to give everything so that our lives may take on real significance—eternal significance—eternal life, the gift of God in Christ to all who will receive it.

Take a moment just now to consider your life from that perspective; see it as a gift from God. Something He wants to last for all eternity. And give your life to Him—with all its questions—and let Him be the answer!

ENDNOTES

1. Victor E. Frankl, *Man's Search for Meaning,* 3rd ed. (New York: Simon & Schuster, 1984), 84.

2. Charles W. Colson, *Loving God* (Grand Rapids, MI: Zondervan, 1983), 172.

Song of Solomon: God's Love Song

What, exactly, is the book we call the Song of Solomon? And what is it doing in the Bible? It, along with Esther, is one of only two books in the entire canon of Scripture that never mention the name of God.

Two thousand years, ago when the Jewish rabbis were disputing which books should be included in the list of books that "defile the hands," both Esther and Song of Solomon were frequently called into question. What, after all, was special about them if God's name wasn't mentioned?

By the way, what the rabbis meant by saying that a book would "defile the hands" is that it was a holy book; and because of that, a person would have to wash his or her hands after touching it.

If you sit down and read this short eight-chapter book, you may find yourself wondering also, *What is this book that describes human love between a man and woman—sometimes in terminology a bit too graphic for polite society—doing in a book of Holy Scripture?*

When I was a young pastor, I took on a special project in the large urban church where I was serving my internship. There was a rebellious teenager named Stan whose mother hoped I could relate to him and bring him back into the church. One night I persuaded Stan to come to an evangelistic meeting. As the preacher presented the timeless truths of Scripture, Stan slouched in his chair, looking bored.

After a few minutes, though, he leaned over to me and asked, "Can I borrow your Bible?"

I was, of course, thrilled. *Aha!* I thought. *Stan is interested! He wants to follow along with the evangelist and look up Bible texts!*

Trying not to let my excitement show, I reached into my suit coat pocket and produced the tiny small-print Bible I always kept there—the one my senior pastor called "a Bible for those under forty." It was a KJV—hardly a modern, youthful translation—but now that my eyes are over forty, I understand what he meant.

Imagine my disappointment when Stan took my Bible and turned immediately to Song of Solomon and began to immerse himself in the one book of the Bible that appealed to his awakening hormones!

"Well, at least he was reading the Bible!" you might say.

But it wasn't exactly what I had hoped for.

Song of Solomon is different from any other book in the Bible. You're probably aware of that, even if you haven't read it recently.

Taken at face value, it appears to be nothing more than a series of love poems.

Through the years many biblical scholars have felt compelled to dig deeper, to try to find some other explanation, some deeper meaning to justify the book's inclusion in the Bible.

> SONG OF SOLOMON IS DIFFERENT FROM ANY OTHER BOOK IN THE BIBLE.

Incidentally, the book is called Song of Solomon not because it was definitely written by Solomon but because Solomon is mentioned several times in it.

"Wait," I hear someone saying, "the book introduces itself this way: 'The song of songs, which is Solomon's' (1:1, KJV). So doesn't that make it plain that Solomon wrote it?"

Well, not really. Scholars point out that the verse could equally mean that the song was written *to* Solomon, *for* Solomon, *in the manner of* Solomon, or *by* Solomon.

The Babylonian Talmud, composed by rabbis in the fifth-century A.D., opined that the book had probably been written or compiled in the time of King Hezekiah.

So, understanding that the book probably wasn't actually written by Solomon, scholars have proposed various ways of interpreting it.

An allegorical interpretation has always been popular. Uncomfortable with the thought that the book might be only about love between a man and woman, Jewish rabbis and church fathers alike suggested that the reason the book merited being included in the Bible was that it was an allegory of God's love for His people.

Sometime in the nineteenth century, other scholars suggested that the book was a drama, and they went to great lengths to interpret it as the story of Solomon and a Shulammite shepherdess.

Other interpreters fabricated a fantastic tale about King Solomon carrying off a Shulammite maiden from her home, against her will. When the young woman resisted his advances, Solomon finally relented and let her return home to the peasant she truly loved.

As exciting as that may seem, there is very little in the book that supports this sort of dramatic reading.

Some Bible students have suggested that the book is a collection of wedding songs, but other scholars disagree with them, pointing out inconsistencies in that theory as well.

I could go on listing theories about what this very different book is and what it's doing in the Bible, but is that really important? The fact of the matter is that Song of Solomon is in the Bible, and we might as well take it at face value. Let it speak for itself, read it as it is, and see what the Lord wants us to learn from it.

Put simply, Song of Solomon is a book about love—the beauty and sacredness of love and admiration between a man and a woman. Take a moment to read this passage from chapter 7 aloud:

> What a magnificent girl you are!
>   How beautiful are your feet in sandals.
> The curve of your thighs
>   is like the work of an artist. . . .
> Your neck is like a tower of ivory.
> Your eyes are like the pools in the city of Heshbon,
>   near the gate of that great city.
> Your nose is as lovely as the tower of Lebanon
>   that stands guard at Damascus.
> Your head is held high like Mount Carmel.
> Your braided hair shines like the finest satin;
>   its beauty could hold a king captive.
> How pretty you are, how beautiful;
>   how complete the delights of your love (verses 1, 4–6, TEV).

That, clearly, is a man's romantically inspired visualization of the love of his life.

The woman, in turn, describes her love like this:

> Like an apple tree among the trees of the forest,
>   so is my dearest compared to other men.
> I love to sit in its shadow,
>   and its fruit is sweet to my taste.
> He brought me to his banquet hall
>   and raised the banner of love over me.
> Restore my strength with raisins
>   and refresh me with apples!
>   I am weak from passion.
> His left hand is under my head,
>   and his right hand caresses me (2:3–6, TEV).

These verses speak unabashedly about beauty and the joy of love between a man and a woman.

Since this poem is more than two thousand years old, its language is sometimes strange to our ears. For example, in chapter 4, the man praises the woman's hair in these words: "Your hair dances like a flock of goats bounding down the hills of Gilead" (verse 1, TEV).

At first glance, that doesn't sound like much of a compliment. How would you like to have someone compare your hair to a flock of goats?

But think of it this way: Imagine a quiet evening. Across the valley, a flock of goats is drifting down the hillside, moving together, flowing like a gentle stream into the valley below. The peacefulness of the scene reminds the man of his lover's hair—restful, flowing, soft.

In chapter 5 the girl describes the man and his hair like this:

> My lover is handsome and strong;
>   he is one in ten thousand.
> His face is bronzed and smooth;
>   his hair is wavy,
>   black as a raven. . . .
> He is majestic, like the Lebanon Mountains,
>   with their towering cedars. . . .
> Everything about him enchants me (verses 10–16a, TEV).

There's a message in these verses, so graphic in their description of physical beauty. Natural love is a *good* thing. It would be unnatural to ignore the beauty of your partner.

Beauty and the ability to appreciate it are gifts from God!

Unfortunately though, the devil has cheapened this expression of beauty. As C. S. Lewis put it:

> You can get a large audience together for a strip-tease act, that is, to watch a girl undress on the stage. Now suppose you came to a country where you could fill a theater by bringing a covered plate onto the stage and then slowly lifting the cover so as to let everyone see, just before the lights went out, that it contained a mutton chop or a bit of bacon, would you not think that in that country something had gone wrong with the appetite for food?[1]

Natural love and greedy lust are two different things—two radically different things.

The Song of Solomon is about love, not lust. When two lovers know their love is a gift from God, when they know their relationship is sacred, they can look at each other and say, "Your beauty is perfect. I love you just the way you are—just because you're you."

This refrain appears over and over in this wonderful love song. In chapter 4 the man describes his lover's beauty for many verses, be-

> THE SONG OF SOLOMON IS ABOUT LOVE, NOT LUST.

ginning with her feet and ending with her hair. Then he concludes, "How beautiful you are, my love; how perfect you are!" (verse 7, TEV).

That's how true love sees its object. True love isn't blind. But it looks for and finds the best in its beloved.

True love is natural, and it's also *romantic*. If you're a woman, wouldn't you like to hear words like these from the man you love?

> The look in your eyes, my sweetheart and bride,
>   and the necklace you are wearing
>   have stolen my heart.
> Your love delights me,
>   my sweetheart and bride.

Your love is better than wine;
>your perfume more fragrant than any spice (verses 9, 10, TEV).

And if you're a man, wouldn't words like these give you a much-appreciated boost to your self-confidence?

There is a fragrance about you;
>the sound of your name recalls it.
>No woman could keep from loving you.
Take me with you, and we'll run away;
>be my king and take me to your room.
We will be happy together,
>drink deep, and lose ourselves in love.
No wonder all women love you! (1:3, 4, TEV).

Whoever wrote the book we call Song of Solomon understood what romance is all about.

Of course, there is more to love than romance.

As C. S. Lewis writes in *Mere Christianity:* "Being in love is a good thing, but it is not the best thing. . . . It is a noble feeling, but it is still a feeling. . . . Who could bear to live in that excitement for even five years?"[2]

"WHO COULD BEAR TO LIVE IN THAT EXCITEMENT FOR EVEN FIVE YEARS?"

The romantic feelings get a relationship started. But a quieter love keeps it going.

Sparks are good at getting fires started; but it's the glowing embers that keep us warm through the night.

And there's another aspect of true love I'd like to consider: true love is *redemptive*.

Early in the Song of Solomon, the young girl says she feels unworthy of being loved.

Don't look down on me because of my color,
>because the sun has tanned me.
My brothers were angry with me
>and made me work in the vineyard.
>I had no time to care for myself (verse 6, TEV).

She feels inadequate. She's had to work out in the vineyards every day and hasn't been able to keep the sun from darkening her complexion—a sure sign in that society that she was from the lower, laboring classes. So she hangs her head and says, "I'm not worthy of your love. I'm not lovable."

But her lover pays no attention to these protests. He is enraptured by her beauty:

> Your hair is beautiful upon your cheeks
> and falls along your neck like jewels. . . .
> How beautiful you are, my love;
> how your eyes shine with love! (verses 10, 15, TEV).

The girl didn't *feel* beautiful; but to her man, she *was* beautiful. And no doubt his words gave her a new sense of confidence.

Redemptive love is like God's love for us. It seeks the best in us and encourages us to build on the positive to achieve even greater things.

Can you think of a better example of love than the cross of Jesus? Look at the cross from God's perspective. He created perfect human beings. But they all sinned, and sin leads to death. So God faced a problem. How could He offer eternal life to sinners who deserved death?

His solution was to offer the death of Jesus as a substitute for the death of every other person who ever lived!

Now that's love! *Redemptive* love. Love extended to people who not only *feel* unworthy but *are* unworthy of such great love and sacrifice.

Redemptive love reaches out, touches, and changes lives.

There is much more we could say about this little book Song of Solomon and what it teaches us about love, but rather than my belaboring the point, why don't you get it out and read it yourself right now?

Remember: it's a picture of human love, but also of the way that God looks at—and loves—you!

ENDNOTES

1. C. S. Lewis, *Mere Christianity* (New York: Macmillan, 1960), 89.

2. Ibid., 99.

CHAPTER 5

Isaiah: Hope in the Ashes

The year: 739 B.C. The place: Jerusalem in the kingdom of Judah. The situation: a nation in distress. On the northern frontier, the larger kingdoms of Syria and Israel have formed a coalition and are planning an attack on Judah. And to the north of them, the powerful Assyrian king, Tiglath-Pileser, is rampaging—overrunning fortresses, raping, pillaging, and torturing his way across the continent, deporting entire nations, carrying the people away from their ancestral homes, and resettling them in foreign lands.

He and his Assyrian army are threatening to move southward at any time, marching through the Promised Land to confront Egypt, Judah's southern neighbor.

It was a time of terror and foreboding the likes of which had never been seen before. For centuries, Israel and Judah had warred among themselves and against other small nations. But no one in all of history had ever encountered a power like the Assyrian war machine.

But it wasn't the Assyrian army that had Isaiah worried. Something else riveted his attention. Something even bigger!

Something with cosmic consequences was on his mind. Here is his description of some-

> NO ONE HAD EVER ENCOUNTERED A POWER LIKE THE ASSYRIAN WAR MACHINE.

thing that had happened to him that struck panic in his heart: "In the year that King Uzziah died, I saw the Lord sitting on a throne, high and lifted up, and the train of His robe filled the temple" (Isaiah 6:1, NKJV).

To Isaiah, encountering the Lord seated on His throne was even more frightening than the prospect of facing the Assyrian killing machine. Isaiah's vision of God's throne room made a deep impression on him, especially because of when it happened: the year of King Uzziah's death.

Do you remember your Bible history? Do you by any chance remember just how King Uzziah died?

Here's the story from 2 Chronicles 26:16: "When [Uzziah] was strong his heart was lifted up, to his destruction, for he transgressed against the LORD his God by entering the temple of the LORD to burn incense" (NKJV).

Uzziah had entered the temple of the Lord—territory that was supposed to be reserved only for sanctified priests. When the high priest tried to stop him from acting rashly, it made the king angry. The Bible continues the story in verses 19, 21:

> Then Uzziah became furious; and he had a censer in his hand to burn incense. And while he was angry with the priests, leprosy broke out on his forehead, before the priests in the house of the LORD, beside the incense altar. . . .
>
> King Uzziah was a leper until the day of his death. He dwelt in an isolated house, because he was a leper; for he was cut off from the house of the LORD. Then Jotham his son was over the king's house, judging the people of the land (NKJV).

King Uzziah—like so many heroes of Greek drama—fell victim to hubris: pride and rebellion against God. And as a result, the Lord struck him with leprosy. He had to turn over the throne to his son Jotham. He died a leper because he failed to have proper respect for the holiness of God.

That puts some perspective on

HE WAS TERRIFIED WHEN HE FOUND HIMSELF STANDING IN THE TEMPLE OF THE LORD.

Isaiah's predicament, doesn't it?

No wonder he was startled—make that terrified—when he found himself standing in the temple of the Lord.

But it wasn't the temple of the Lord in Jerusalem that Isaiah found himself in. In his vision, he found himself in the very throne room of God in heaven!

If Uzziah had died for entering the throne room of God on earth, what would happen to a sinful person who entered the throne room of God in heaven?

No wonder Isaiah cried out in fear, "Woe is me, for I am ruined! Because I am a man of unclean lips, and I live among a people of unclean lips; for my eyes have seen the King, the LORD of hosts" (Isaiah 6:5, NASB).

Isaiah was a prophet of God. He spoke for the Lord and was accustomed to listening for the voice of the Lord. But to go into the Lord's very presence! That was an entirely different matter.

He knew he wasn't holy enough to be there, and he feared for his life. Wouldn't you, considering what had happened to King Uzziah?

The good news, of course, is that Isaiah had nothing to fear from his gracious God. He hadn't barged into God's presence; he'd been invited there by God Himself! And so God ministered His grace to Isaiah. Notice what happened next:

> Then one of the seraphim flew to me, having in his hand a live coal which he had taken with the tongs from the altar. And he touched my mouth with it, and said: "Behold, this has touched your lips; your iniquity is taken away, and your sin purged" (verses 6, 7, NKJV).

In his own righteousness Isaiah had no right to be in the heavenly temple—anymore than King Uzziah had the right to be in the temple in Jerusalem. But God Himself had invited Isaiah there—at least in vision. And so, instead of striking him with leprosy, God sent an angel to offer Isaiah what he needed in order to stand in the presence of a Holy God: Cleansing. Forgiveness. Purging.

Isaiah came away from his encounter with God with something very different than what Uzziah received—because Isaiah showed humility in God's presence, while King Uzziah had gone into the temple with defiant pride.

Uzziah received a death sentence.

Isaiah received a life sentence.

Isaiah was given the opportunity to live out his life as God's spokesman, to bring messages from the Lord to His people.

It wouldn't be an easy task, because most of the people didn't really want to hear God's word. They were content with the way things were and didn't want to be challenged to follow God's ways more closely.

Still Isaiah appealed to them, in the poignant words we know from chapter 1, verse 18:

"Come now, and let us reason together,"
Says the LORD,
"Though your sins are like scarlet,
They shall be as white as snow;
Though they are red like crimson,
They shall be as wool" (NKJV).

The Lord came to His people offering the same sort of blessing He gave to Isaiah. "Sure, you're sinful," He says. "But I have a cure for that. You can be cleansed just like Isaiah was, if you'll come to Me. Here's how you can do it: 'Wash yourselves, make yourselves clean; put away the evil of your doings from before My eyes. Cease to do evil, learn to do good; seek justice, rebuke the oppressor; defend the fatherless, plead for the widow' " (verses 16, 17, NKJV).

This theme is repeated over and over throughout Isaiah's prophecies. Much of the book consists of descriptions of the dire consequences of failure to respond in humility to God. And when the question of what God really wants from His people comes up, Isaiah often decries the injustice and lack of love in the land. "Your rulers are rebels, and companions of thieves; everyone loves a bribe, and chases after rewards. They do not defend the orphan, nor does the widow's plea come before them," he says in Isaiah 1:23 (NASB).

"What do you mean by crushing My people and grinding the face of the poor?" he asks in Isaiah 3:15 (NASB).

"Woe to those who enact evil statutes and to those who constantly record unjust decisions, so as to deprive the needy of justice and rob the poor of My people of their rights, so that widows may be their spoil and that they may plunder the orphans," he proclaims in Isaiah 10:1, 2 (NASB).

ISAIAH LIVED THROUGH ONE OF THE GREATEST RELIGIOUS REFORMATIONS IN HISTORY.

Yes, a lot of the book of Isaiah consists of proclamations of woe upon the people because of the injustice in the land.

And what makes this especially significant is the fact that Isaiah lived through one of the greatest religious reformations in the history of the kingdom of Judah—in the days of good King Hezekiah.

When Hezekiah took the throne, he called people back to worshiping the Lord. He ordered the temple cleaned out, removed the

Assyrian altar his father had installed, and sponsored a huge feast, at which the people brought sacrifices and offerings to the Lord.

Second Chronicles 29:32–34 describes a religious festival so huge that the priests couldn't keep up with their duties: "The number of the burnt offerings which the assembly brought was seventy bulls, one hundred rams, and two hundred lambs; all these were for a burnt offering to the LORD. The consecrated things were six hundred bulls and three thousand sheep. But the priests were too few, so that they could not skin all the burnt offerings" (NKJV).

> ISAIAH SAW THROUGH THE RELIGIOUS VENEER TO THE ROUGH UNDERSIDE OF THEIR LIVES.

What a mammoth celebration of sacrifice! What an amazing new consecration of the people to worshiping the Lord.

But even though the people returned to "church," as it were—and celebrated great sacrifices and Passover feasts—Isaiah saw through the religious veneer to the rough underside of their lives. And he never ceased calling people to the kind of genuine heart religion that would demonstrate itself in justice and love to the downtrodden.

In the very first chapter of his prophetic message, Isaiah confronts the religiosity of the people:

> What to me is the multitude of your sacrifices?
>   says the LORD;
> I have had enough of burnt offerings of rams
>   and the fat of fed beasts;
> I do not delight in the blood of bulls,
>   or of lambs, or of goats.
> When you come to appear before me,
>   who asked this from your hand?
>   Trample my courts no more;
> bringing offerings is futile;
>   incense is an abomination to me.
> New moon and sabbath and calling of convocation—
>   I cannot endure solemn assemblies with iniquity
>   (Isaiah 1:11–13, NRSV).

Religious ceremony, sacrifice, and celebration weren't what God wanted most from His people. No, what He wanted was true religion:

Learn to do good;
    seek justice,
        rescue the oppressed,
    defend the orphan,
        plead for the widow (verse 17, NRSV).

" 'If you are willing and obedient, you shall eat the good of the land,' " he promised. " 'But if you refuse and rebel, you shall be devoured by the sword'; for the mouth of the LORD has spoken" (verses 19, 20, NKJV).

Unfortunately, Isaiah's message fell mostly on deaf ears. Because the people didn't respond, his predictions of doom came true for most of the kingdom of Judah.

At one point, every fortified city in the country except Jerusalem was conquered by Assyrian armies. Thousands were devoured by the sword, and thousands more were sold into slavery.

But Isaiah also looked beyond the gloom and doom to a better time. The last twenty-seven chapters of the book looked forward to a time when God would restore rather than tear down. They begin with these familiar words:

> Comfort ye, comfort ye my people, saith your God. Speak ye comfortably to Jerusalem, and cry unto her, that her warfare is accomplished, that her iniquity is pardoned: for she hath received of the LORD's hand double for all her sins (Isaiah 40:1, 2, KJV).

EVERY FORTIFIED CITY IN THE COUNTRY EXCEPT JERUSALEM WAS CONQUERED BY ASSYRIAN ARMIES.

These verses are the prelude to the great promise of the coming of the Messiah—the words that John the Baptist quoted seven centuries later in the Judean wilderness: "The voice of him that crieth in the wilderness, Prepare ye the way of the LORD, make straight in the desert a highway for our God" (verse 3, KJV).

The following chapters include the precious promises about the Suffering Servant who would bear our sins and minister God's grace to us.

He was wounded for our transgressions,
    crushed for our iniquities;

upon him was the punishment that made us whole,
and by his bruises we are healed (Isaiah 53:5, NRSV).

And Jesus, the Suffering-Servant Messiah, read from the scroll of Isaiah at the beginning of His ministry:

The scroll of the prophet Isaiah was given to him. He unrolled the scroll and found the place where it was written:

"The Spirit of the Lord is upon me,
because he has anointed me
to bring good news to the poor.
He has sent me to proclaim release to the captives
and recovery of sight to the blind,
to let the oppressed go free,
to proclaim the year of the Lord's favor"
(Luke 4:17–19, NRSV).

Isaiah's message is for those living now as well. The Lord still comes to us today, with His appeal: Come, let us reason together. The Lord still appeals to us to let Him wash us and make us clean. And He still cries out on behalf of the poor and downtrodden, pleading their case and asking us as Christians to be His representatives in helping them.

Religion such as the people experienced in the early days of Hezekiah's reign—coming together for a celebration and feast—is one thing. But the true religious experience that God wanted for His people was the same in Isaiah's day as it was when the apostle James wrote to Christians: "Religion that is pure and undefiled before God, the Father, is this: to care for orphans and widows in their distress, and to keep oneself unstained by the world" (James 1:27, NRSV).

Isaiah found himself in the presence of God. He didn't feel worthy to be there, but God cleansed his lips, gave him a message for his people, and empowered him to call people to true religion characterized by deeds of mercy.

God still calls us—you and me—to come to Him. He still offers us cleansing.

And He still invites us to go on missions of mercy to the world.

CHAPTER 6

Jeremiah: A Call to Heart Religion

I magine yourself in Jeremiah's sandals for a moment. You're a young person—maybe a teenager. You live in a little village about an hour's walk from your nation's capital. From a spot just down the road, you can look south toward Jerusalem and see the gleaming white walls of Solomon's glorious temple that has stood as a center of worship of the Lord for more than three centuries.

You're about the same age as the boy king Josiah, who found himself on the throne of Judah at the age of eight, after his father was assassinated.

The village where you live is well-known as the home of a family of priests who can trace their lineage clear back to the time of Israel's greatest kings, David and Solomon.

In fact, if you remember the stories from the book of 1 Kings about the transition of power from King David to King Solomon, perhaps you remember that Solomon's brother Adonijah tried to take the throne against his father's will, and that a priest by the name of Abiathar supported Adonijah in his rebellion. In Solomon's view, Abiathar deserved to die for his disloyalty, but instead of having him killed, Solomon had him banished to Anathoth, the village of the priests.

INSTEAD OF HAVING HIM KILLED, SOLOMON HAD HIM BANISHED TO ANATHOTH.

Three-and-a-half centuries later, your hometown, Anathoth, is still a village of priests. And you, Jeremiah, are just a young fellow, living out your *Mayberry R.F.D.* lifestyle, far enough removed from the seat of power that you never expect to personally meet the king or any of the high officials of the country, when suddenly everything changes.

Lately, exciting news has been circulating around your town. King Josiah—who's now about twenty years old—has had a spiritual awakening! He's calling on people throughout the country to put away their foreign gods and come to Jerusalem to celebrate a great Passover feast to the Lord. Heralds have carried invitations throughout the land, and even into Assyrian-held territory to the north, in the former kingdom of Israel.

There is a new sense of religious fervor in the land! People are being called upon to return to worshiping the Lord with their whole hearts.

Josiah's father, grandfather, and great-great-grandfather had felt compelled by their Assyrian overlords to give allegiance to the Assyrian gods, along with the Lord. His great-great-grandfather Ahaz had even erected an Assyrian altar in the temple in Jerusalem!

Only Josiah's great-grandfather (Ahaz's son) Hezekiah had dared to take a strong stand against Assyria. And he had done so at great cost. His entire nation had been overrun and pillaged by the rapacious Assyrian war machine. Only Jerusalem was spared from the near-total annihilation that engulfed the rest of the country; and that deliverance came about only by the miraculous intervention of the angel of the Lord (see 2 Chronicles 32; Isaiah 37).

But now the Assyrian Empire is waning in power, and King Josiah is calling on the people to abandon their foreign gods and worship only the Lord, much as Hezekiah had done.

YOU EXPECT GREAT THINGS FROM THE REIGN OF THIS SPIRITUALLY ENLIGHTENED RULER.

That sounds like great news! As a member of a priestly family, you can't help but rejoice and expect great things from the reign of this spiritually enlightened ruler.

Then it happens.

One day when you're all alone, the word of the Lord comes to you: "Jeremiah . . . Jeremiah . . . *Jeremiah*!"

"Yes, Lord?"

"Jeremiah, I want you to know that you are no stranger to Me. In fact, I've been watching you—since even before you were born. And long ago, I chose you to be a prophet to speak My words to kings and kingdoms—to declare which ones will be built up and which ones will be torn down."

Wow! Sounds pretty exciting, doesn't it? To be given that kind of authority as a teenager.

But apparently Jeremiah wasn't too enthusiastic about it. He reminded the Lord that he was just a young lad who hadn't taken Public Speaking 101 in college yet—in fact, he'd never even been to a Toastmasters meeting.

But the Lord insisted. "Do not say, 'I am a youth,' " He said. "For you shall go to all to whom I send you, and whatever I command you, you shall speak" (Jeremiah 1:7, NKJV).

GOD IS STILL PREDICTING TROUBLE FROM THE NORTH? WHY?

"OK, OK," I can hear Jeremiah saying. After all, how can you argue with God when He comes to you? "So, what am I supposed to say to the people?"

Then it happens. You have your first vision. An odd vision at that—all you see is a branch of an almond tree. What can it mean?

And then the Lord explains—and there's a neat little play on words in the Hebrew here—based on the fact that the almond is the first tree to blossom in the spring, and people tended to watch their almond trees as they looked forward to the end of winter. The Lord explains the vision like this: Jeremiah says to the Lord, "I see the rod of a *watch-tree*," and the Lord explains, "I am *watching* over My word to fulfill it."

Now, at first glance you'd think that the Lord's opening message to Jeremiah was a prediction of great joy, that the almond branch—harbinger of spring—must represent the wonderful rebirth of genuine worship in the kingdom.

But notice what happened next: "And the word of the LORD came to me the second time, saying, 'What do you see?' And I said, 'I see a boiling pot, and it is facing away from the north.' Then the LORD said to me: 'Out of the north calamity shall break forth on all the inhabitants of the land' " (verses 13, 14, NKJV).

A little geography lesson might help here. The kingdom of Judah was located in Palestine. To the north lay the route to Assyria and Babylon, and to the south lay Egypt. So now God is predicting that trouble is going to come from the north.

What? Just when Assyria's power is waning and religious revival has broken out in the land, God is still predicting trouble from the north? Why?

When you read the book of Jeremiah, you'll notice that most of his prophecies are predictions of disaster.

Jeremiah's mission was to call the people to true repentance, to true heart religion. And to help them understand that when disasters came upon them, it was because they hadn't trusted fully in the Lord.

Oh, yes, there had been reforms under Josiah. But the people's hearts weren't truly reformed. They attended great religious festivals, but it didn't change their underlying attitude.

Much like Isaiah before him, Jeremiah's mission was to call them to genuine loyalty to the Lord, not just to religiosity.

And for the next forty years, this was the burden resting on Jeremiah's heart. Burning there so intensely that even when he tried to keep silent, he just couldn't do it. Sometimes he decided not to speak anymore in the name of the Lord; but when he did, he had to admit that "[the Lord's] word was in my heart like a burning fire shut up in my bones; I was weary of holding it back, and I could not" (Jeremiah 20:9, NKJV).

But there was more to Jeremiah's message than just a warning that calamity was coming from the north. There was a reason for all this trouble. (And by the way, the Lord's original message proved true. Even though the Assyrian Empire to the north soon collapsed, a new northern kingdom—Babylon—was waiting in the wings to bring the Lord's judgments down on the land.)

YOU COULDN'T STOP PEOPLE FROM CLIMBING A ONCE-SACRED HILL.

The reason for it was simple but deep seated.

Because, you see, despite young King Josiah's good intentions, the people were not turning wholeheartedly back to the Lord. Oh, sure, they were willing to participate when there was a big religious celebration like the Passover. But they would leave that spiritual high point and go back to their humdrum daily lives in little villages and farming communities all over the land, and when things didn't go well—when there was a drought or a killing frost too late in the spring—their thoughts would immediately turn to the ways of their ancestors and the ways of their non-Hebrew neighbors. And they'd find themselves up at the temples on the high places throughout the land, participating in the licentious worship exercises there and appealing to foreign gods.

King Josiah had torn down most of the temples and altars at those high places, but you couldn't stop people from climbing a once-sacred hill and calling out to the gods that had been worshiped there from time immemorial.

Their hearts were still with the old ways that had become popular when Josiah's ancestors had capitulated to the Assyrians. Years later, after Jerusalem had fallen to the Babylonians, the survivors who fled to Egypt told Jeremiah that they blamed him—along with King Josiah—for their troubles. They thought that calamity had come upon them because they had quit worshiping the foreign gods!

THEY HAD EVIDENCE THAT FOCUSING WORSHIP ON JUDAH'S GOD HAD BROUGHT DISASTER ON THE LAND.

Jeremiah 44:16–18 reveals their attitude. When Jeremiah appealed to them to worship the Lord, they responded by saying that they were abandoning the worship of the Lord and returning to worship of other gods such as the Canaanite goddess known as the Queen of Heaven:

> "As for the word that you have spoken to us in the name of the LORD, we will not listen to you! But we will certainly do whatever has gone out of our own mouth, to burn incense to the queen of heaven and pour out drink offerings to her, as we have done, we and our fathers, our kings and our princes, in the cities of Judah and in the streets of Jerusalem. For then we had plenty of food, were well-off, and saw no trouble. But since we stopped burning incense to the queen of heaven and pouring out drink offerings to her, we have lacked everything and have been consumed by the sword and by famine" (NKJV).

They claimed they had empirical evidence that focusing worship on Judah's God and neglecting the foreign gods had brought disaster on the land. And so the people turned their backs on the Lord even more stubbornly and devoted themselves to other gods.

And most horrible, their religion of choice—the religion practiced up on those sacred mountains—involved human sacrifice! They didn't just go up on the mountains to pray. Here's Jeremiah's description of their worship:

"They have forsaken Me and made this an alien place, because they have burned incense in it to other gods whom neither they, their fathers, nor the kings of Judah have known, and have filled this place with the blood of the innocents. They have also built the high places of Baal, *to burn their sons with fire for burnt offerings to Baal*" (Jeremiah 19:4, 5, NKJV; emphasis added).

What could make people continue to believe in and return to such a horrific form of worship?

The fact is that those high places continued to be a snare, not only because the people thought it would protect them from their enemies, but because the religion practiced there had an excitement about it that they didn't sense in the staid ceremonies at the temple in Jerusalem.

Jeremiah knew what went on up there: "Truly the hills are a delusion, the *orgies on the mountains*. Truly in the LORD our God is the salvation of Israel," he declared (Jeremiah 3:23, NRSV; emphasis added).

> THE ULTIMATE DISASTER CAME BOILING OUT OF THE NORTH.

People in Jeremiah's day were not irreligious. They had a lot of religion. But it wasn't heart religion. It wasn't the kind of religion that changed the way they treated their neighbors, and Jeremiah delivered his messages of judgment because of that. The Lord sadly described His people in these words: "They have grown fat, they are sleek; yes, they surpass the deeds of the wicked; they do not plead the cause, the cause of the fatherless; yet they prosper, and the right of the needy they do not defend" (Jeremiah 5:28, NKJV).

Sadly, Jeremiah's words of judgment came all too true. Less than twenty years after Jeremiah's first vision, King Nebuchadnezzar of Babylon deposed Israel's king and put his own puppet on the throne. This was after Josiah's disastrous attack on Pharaoh Necho, described in volume 1 in the chapter on 2 Kings (see 2 Kings 23).

Then, just forty years after Jeremiah's vision of the seething pot about to spill out over the land, the ultimate disaster came boiling out of the north as Babylonian armies encircled Jerusalem, broke down its walls, and burned every beautiful house, including the Lord's temple, to the ground!

All because the people did not turn with their whole hearts to the Lord. These poignant words describe God's will for His people:

> "Behold, the days are coming, says the LORD, when I will make a new covenant with the house of Israel and with the house of Judah. . . . I will put My law in their minds, and write it on their hearts; and I will be their God, and they shall be My people. No more shall every man teach his neighbor, and every man his brother, saying, 'Know the LORD,' for they all shall know Me, from the least of them to the greatest of them, says the LORD. For I will forgive their iniquity, and their sin I will remember no more" (Jeremiah 31:31–34, NKJV).

That's what God wanted all along for His people. That their religion would be something deep down in their hearts that didn't only make them feel good or get them excited at a great feast day. But a religion that changed their hearts and made them willing subjects of His law, willing helpers and lovers of their neighbors—people who tended to the needs of the poor, the orphans, and widows.

And that is still what God wants for His people today. The New Testament book of Hebrews picks up Jeremiah's refrain, quoting the entire passage about the new covenant in chapter 8.

God wanted His people to be good, true, loving people in Jeremiah's day. And that's what He wants for us today as well!

He invites you to take time today, and every day, to invite Him deep down into your heart. To ask Him what difference heart religion would make in what you do and say today, and to live out your religion in the way you treat others and meet the needs of the unfortunate.

He wants to put His law, His will, His love, deep down inside you, where it will bubble over and change your life—and the lives of those around you!

CHAPTER 7

Lamentations: Jeremiah's Sorrow

You've been there, haven't you—the place where nothing seems to make sense anymore, where all your hopes and dreams have come crumbling down in a heap, and you wonder what's the point of going on?

Jeremiah faced a time like that. Things had been going from bad to worse for him for a long time, and now they were to the point where it didn't seem they could get any lower. He'd spent time in prison and had been moved from there to a hole in the ground with mud at the bottom—into which he sank.

By the way, if you've heard the story about Jeremiah and the cistern, perhaps you remember hearing this verse: "They took Jeremiah and threw him into the cistern of Malchiah, the king's son, which was in the court of the guard, letting Jeremiah down by ropes. Now there was no water in the cistern, but only mud, and Jeremiah sank in the mud" (Jeremiah 38:6, NRSV).

IT WAS A REMINDER OF THE DISASTROUS CONDITIONS BROUGHT UPON THE CITY.

Typically when we hear that story, our emphasis is on poor Jeremiah, sinking down in the mud. But to the original readers of the story, the imagery that probably stuck with them was that of an empty cistern, which no longer held drinking water. To them it was a reminder of the disastrous conditions brought upon the city by the besieging Babylonian army.

It was a condition that had resulted from a long series of wrong choices on both the spiritual and political levels.

For nearly forty years, Jeremiah had been appealing to the people and the political leaders of the city to commit their ways to the Lord rather than relying on their own strength.

The Lord had revealed to Jeremiah—on the day that He called him to his prophetic mission—that the Babylonians would be like a pot of boiling water spilling down from the north, a seething tsunami engulfing everything in its path, and that unless His people repented, they would be victims of the Babylonian onslaught.

But rather than heed Jeremiah's warnings, the people had continued in their rebellious ways, and now they were ready to "shoot the messenger" rather than accept his message.

> NOW THEY WERE READY TO "SHOOT THE MESSENGER" RATHER THAN ACCEPT HIS MESSAGE.

Because of their continued rebellion, things kept getting worse and worse.

The day soon came when there wasn't a single loaf of bread left in the city—even the king and his nobles were on starvation rations.

Then finally on July 19, 586 B.C., the Babylonian army breached the walls, marched into the city, and took all the leading citizens captive—shipping the most prominent off to Syria, where they were summarily executed (see 2 Kings 25:1–21).

King Zedekiah thought he could outsmart his enemies. Apparently he had a secret passageway out of the city. The book of 2 Kings describes his desperate attempt to save himself and his army, and the disastrous result:

> Then the city wall was broken through, and all the men of war fled at night by way of the gate between two walls, which was by the king's garden. . . . But the army of the Chaldeans pursued the king, and they overtook him in the plains of Jericho. . . . So they took the king and brought him up to the king of Babylon at Riblah, and they pronounced judgment on him. Then they killed the sons of Zedekiah before his eyes, put out the eyes of Zedekiah, bound him with bronze fetters, and took him to Babylon (2 Kings 25:4–7, NKJV).

What a horrible fate! The last thing the king saw was his sons being killed before his eyes!

Back in Jerusalem, you can hear the siege survivors trying to look on the bright side: "Things have got to get better soon—they can't get any worse!"

But things did get worse. A month after the city was captured, the order went out to the occupying forces: Burn the place to the ground. Every building. The temple! The house of the Lord! The king's palace. Every building. Even the beggars' hovels. Burn them all down. Don't leave a wall standing anywhere. Turn Jerusalem into a rubbish heap.

No wonder Jeremiah penned words like these, found in Lamentations 2:11:

> My eyes are spent with weeping;
> my stomach churns;
> my bile is poured out on the ground
> because of the destruction of my people (NRSV).

The power of the story in Lamentations is heightened by its poetic form and raw imagery.

The first four chapters of this five-chapter book are written in a poetic form that amplifies the sense of grief portrayed in the imagery. As *The Seventh-day Adventist Bible Commentary* points out:

> In the Hebrew the book of Lamentations exhibits a unique poetic structure: its metrical system is that of the *qinah* rhythm. . . . [E]ach line has five beats, three in the first half and two in the second half, giving the effect of a long crescendo followed by a shorter decrescendo, as if grief rises to its height and then spends itself more quickly. Moreover, the whole poem is an extended example of *qinah* rhythm, in that the dirge mounts to its height in chapter 3 and more quickly descends to its base level at the end of chapter 5.[1]

THE IMAGERY IS LAID OUT WITH FRANKNESS NOT WITNESSED ANYWHERE ELSE IN THE BIBLE.

The imagery of what had happened to Jerusalem as a result of its failure to respond to Jeremiah's prophetic messages is laid out with frankness not witnessed anywhere else in the Bible. Lamentations 1:9, 10 pictures the disaster as a rape:

> IT IS HARD TO READ THESE WORDS WITHOUT CHOKING UP.

Her uncleanness is in her skirts;
She did not consider her destiny; . . .
The adversary has spread his hand
Over all her pleasant things;
For she has seen the nations enter her sanctuary,
Those whom You commanded
Not to enter Your assembly (NKJV).

Jeremiah recalls in word-pictures the days of the city's demise:

"My priests and my elders
Breathed their last in the city,
While they sought food
To restore their life" (verse 19, NKJV).

Young men, the pride of the nation, have been dashed to pieces and left like broken potsherds in the streets:

The precious sons of Zion,
Valuable as fine gold,
How they are regarded as clay pots,
The work of the hands of the potter! (Lamentations 4:2, NKJV).

Young mothers have been reduced to the most desperate state imaginable:

The hands of the compassionate women
Have cooked their own children;
They became food for them
In the destruction of the daughter of my people
(verse 10, NKJV).

It is hard to read these words and visualize the events without choking up.

But what made the tragedy even worse was that it all could have been avoided.

Grief counselors tell us that playing "What if" is a natural part of dealing with tragedy: "What if we'd just taken a different street? What if we'd tried a different doctor or natural remedy? What if . . ."

But by the time we're playing that game, it's too late to do anything differently.

For Jeremiah, the question that must have run through his mind was, *What if people had just listened and responded to the warning messages I gave? Could I have done something more to get their attention and motivate them to change their ways?* He knew that

THINGS COULD HAVE ENDED DIFFERENTLY IF THE PEOPLE HAD BEEN WILLING.

things could have ended differently if the people had been willing to listen and repent of their sins. Perhaps he was burdened with a feeling of guilt: *What if I'd tried a little harder to persuade the king to take the Lord's course?*

Perhaps the greatest temptation to a prophet whose words of warning haven't been heeded is to simply stand back and look at the resulting destruction and say, "I told you so!" and to stalk off the scene to let people suffer the consequences.

But Jeremiah didn't do that. In fact, the Babylonian ruler who was left in charge after Jerusalem was destroyed gave Jeremiah a choice—either he could go with a group of exiles who were being deported to Babylon, or he could stay in his own ruined country. Even given the opportunity to leave behind the nightmare into which he had been dragged, Jeremiah chose to stick it out and stay with the very people who had caused the calamity.

He stood faithfully beside those who were suffering the consequences of not listening to him!

What a courageous man he was.

And how poignantly his book of Lamentations portrays the sorrow that came upon God's people as a result of their stubborn rebellion.

Thinking of how joyful the city had once been when pilgrims would come, singing down the highway through his hometown of Anathoth on their way to festivals, he wrote:

The roads to Zion mourn
Because no one comes to the set feasts.

All her gates are desolate;
Her priests sigh,
Her virgins are afflicted,
And she is in bitterness (Lamentations 1:4, NKJV).

Remembering the day when the city fell to the Babylonians, he pictures the distress of the king's sons as they tried desperately to out-run the Babylonian cavalry, accompanied by the tattered remnants of their father's once-proud army:

Her princes have become like deer
That find no pasture,
That flee without strength
Before the pursuer (verse 6, NKJV).

Jeremiah remembers with horror the sight of enemy soldiers going into the Most Holy Place in the temple—defiling it and robbing it of its treasures—and pleads with his God:

"See, O LORD, and consider!
To whom have You done this?
Should the women eat their offspring,
The children they have cuddled?
Should the priest and prophet be slain
In the sanctuary of the Lord?" (Lamentations 2:20, NKJV).

NOW THE SOUNDS HE REMEMBERS COMING FROM THE TEMPLE ARE NOT THE JOYOUS SHOUTS OF FESTIVAL.

He remembers with a touch of nostalgia the time when he heard joyous shouts coming from the temple at the annual festivals. But now:

The Lord has spurned His altar,
He has abandoned His sanctuary;
He has given up the walls of her palaces
Into the hand of the enemy.
They have made a noise in the house of the LORD
As on the day of a set feast (verse 7, NKJV).

Now the sounds he remembers coming from the temple are not the joyous shouts of festival, but screams of terror and the raucous shouts of soldiers bullying, looting, and killing.

These tragedies all came upon Jerusalem, and Jeremiah witnessed them with his own eyes, and described them in Lamentations' powerful word-pictures:

> The elders of the daughter of Zion
> Sit on the ground and keep silence;
> They throw dust on their heads
> And gird themselves with sackcloth.
> The virgins of Jerusalem
> Bow their heads to the ground (verse 10, NKJV).

> Those who ate delicacies
> Are desolate in the streets;
> Those who were brought up in scarlet
> Embrace ash heaps (Lamentations 4:5, NKJV).

The imagery in Lamentations really brings home the tragedy that the people of Jerusalem suffered. You can see it, can't you—a teenage boy who was raised in the lap of luxury, walking through the city, begging for food, then finally wandering back to the street where he once played with his friends, stumbling down the road to the gate of what was a beautiful manor, and falling on his face, cling-

> A TEENAGE BOY FALLING ON HIS FACE, CLINGING TO THE ASHES THAT ARE ALL THAT IS LEFT.

ing to the ashes that are all that is left of the place he called home.

It's like a nightmare to Jeremiah, but it is the reality he must face every day of his life from now on. The people didn't listen. And the Judgment Day finally came.

But amazingly, the book of Lamentations also includes some glimmers of hope. Here's a familiar passage you've probably heard, but you might not have realized it came from Lamentations.

> Through the LORD's mercies we are not consumed,
> Because His compassions fail not.
> They are new every morning;

Great is Your faithfulness.
"The LORD is my portion," says my soul,
"Therefore I hope in Him!"
The LORD is good to those who wait for Him,
To the soul who seeks Him.
It is good that one should hope and wait quietly
For the salvation of the LORD (Lamentations 3:22–26, NKJV).

So, what can we learn from this poetic look at the sorrow—and hope—of God's prophet in a time of despair? Much.

We can learn much from the example of Jeremiah, who faithfully delivered the word of the Lord, even though it made him the most unpopular man in the city, and finally landed him in jail. His example in staying the course and standing by his people all through their tragedy—even though the disaster was a result of not listening to him—is worthy of emulation.

There's another lesson, too, in the picture of the desolation suffered in those days. People in Jeremiah's day no doubt responded to his repeated warnings of the judgments of the Lord by saying "Oh, yeah, we've heard all that before—prophets have been saying that kind of thing for generations, but it never happens!"

People still respond that way when we talk about the prophecies of the second coming of Jesus, don't they? There's a warning here in the book of Lamentations.

But there's also hope. It *is* a good thing to wait for the Lord, for our souls to be drawn out to seek Him every day. It *is* a good thing to hope and quietly wait for the salvation of the Lord. Whatever our circumstances. For His salvation will come. If not right away, then at the second coming of Jesus.

Lamentations isn't the most pleasant book of the Bible to study. But it's there for our learning and admonition. It takes just a few minutes to read. In reading it, we may weep with the prophet, but we may also grow in our faith and in our trust that God will stand beside us in both our sorrow and our joy.

ENDNOTE

1. Francis D. Nichol, ed., *The Seventh-day Adventist Bible Commentary* (Washington DC: Review and Herald® Publishing Association, 1977), 3:19.

CHAPTER 8 _____

Ezekiel: Hope for the Future

When you think of the prophet Ezekiel, what comes to mind? Is it the four-faced beasts flying around with wheels chasing them, described in chapter 1? Or does your mind run immediately to Ezekiel's famous vision of the valley full of dry bones? Or maybe when you think of Ezekiel, it reminds you of his prophecies about Gog and Magog.

Ezekiel is forty-eight chapters long, and it includes a wide (sometimes wild) variety of prophecies, some of them rather strange-sounding. So in this chapter I want to focus on one aspect that draws the entire book together—the message that God wants to put His Spirit into His people and give them new lives.

But in order to understand why this message was so important at the time that it was given, let's take a moment to consider the book's historical background.

Ezekiel had his first vision in 593 B.C., four years after he—along with much of the leadership of the kingdom of Judah—had been deported from Jerusalem to Babylon. (This was eight years after the time when Daniel was taken to Babylon.)

There had been a lot of conflict in Jerusalem in the dozen years leading up to 597. Back in 609 B.C., the great king Josiah had marched his army out of the city to try to stop the Egyptian army from passing through his territory to fight against the Babylonians. But in the ensuing battle, King Josiah died.

> EZEKIEL INCLUDES A WIDE (SOMETIMES WILD) VARIETY OF PROPHECIES.

His son Jehoahaz then took the throne, but three months later Pharaoh came and took Jehoahaz captive and put Jehoahaz's brother Jehoiakim on the throne as a tribute-paying vassal.

A few years later, though, the Babylonian king Nebuchadnezzar chased the Egyptians out of Judah, and King Jehoiakim had to switch allegiance and begin paying tribute to the Babylonians. For a few years, he walked a tightrope between Egypt and Babylon, but finally he jumped off the rope and declared his independence.

Then at the end of 598 B.C., Nebuchadnezzar's army marched out of Babylon on a mission to show Jehoiakim who was boss. Jehoiakim died about that time, and his son Jehoiachin took the throne. Some historians theorize that Jehoiakim may have been killed in a coup perpetrated by those who knew better than to resist the Babylonian onslaught (perhaps those who trusted Jeremiah's prophetic message).

Nebuchadnezzar's army besieged Jerusalem in March of 597 B.C., and Jehoiachin proved wiser than his father. Rather than continuing the rebellion, "Jehoiachin king of Judah, his mother, his servants, his princes, and his officers went out to the king of Babylon; and the king of Babylon, in the eighth year of his reign, took him prisoner" (2 Kings 24:12, NKJV).

While this wise move spared the city from destruction, the leaders obviously did not get off scot-free. Many of them were taken in chains to Babylon. Ezekiel must have been among those carried captive away from their homeland at that time.

> EZEKIEL MUST HAVE BEEN AMONG THOSE CARRIED CAPTIVE AWAY FROM THEIR HOMELAND.

Incidentally, the date when Jehoiachin surrendered to Babylon is recorded in Babylonian cuneiform records, and "is the most exact information to come from cuneiform records for an event recorded in the Bible, and gives us a precise date for the fall of Jerusalem in the capture of Jehoiachin." That exact date is March 16, 597 B.C.[1]

Four years later, God called Ezekiel to be a prophet—to deliver divine messages to the captives in Babylon as well as to the people who had stayed in Jerusalem.

Meanwhile, back in Jerusalem, the prophet Jeremiah was calling the people to repent of their sins, lest something worse come upon them. But no one paid much attention. They thought everything was fine with them. In fact, they thought that God's judgments had already been poured out, and that since they hadn't been carried away into exile, they were the ones God had chosen as His faithful remnant, who would be allowed to stay in the land. They wouldn't believe Jeremiah when he told them they still needed to repent and turn with their whole hearts to the Lord.

So, that was the situation when God called Ezekiel.

Ezekiel's prophecies, coming from one who was already suffering in Babylonian captivity, were like an exclamation point added to the messages of Jeremiah. Ezekiel saw amazing things and delivered astounding messages—often acting out parables in ways calculated to startle his audience.

Unfortunately, most people still didn't pay much attention. They continued their rebellion against God and against the Babylonians, and because of that, both Jeremiah's and Ezekiel's warnings of disaster to come became more and more strident.

Finally, a time came when it seemed all hope was lost.

But, even in those dire circumstances, God called His prophet Ezekiel to inspire people with hope for the future.

> MAYBE YOU'D EVEN BE TEMPTED TO TAKE THE "EAT DRINK AND BE MERRY" ATTITUDE.

Perhaps the hopelessness of the situation during the early years of Ezekiel's ministry is best summed up in chapter 21, verse 4, where the Lord reveals that things in Judah have gotten so bad that He is bringing judgment that will spare no one, neither the righteous nor the wicked. Here's the word of the Lord as revealed to Ezekiel: "I will cut off both righteous and wicked from you, therefore My sword shall go out of its sheath against all flesh from south to north" (Ezekiel 21:4, NKJV).

If you were one of the residents of Jerusalem who heard a prophecy like that, how would that make you feel? Wouldn't it leave you feeling hopeless?

Maybe you'd even be tempted to take the "eat drink and be merry" attitude, thinking it didn't matter what you did from then on, because it wouldn't make any difference.

But let's take a moment to put this discouraging prophecy in context. It came from Ezekiel, the same prophet who just a year earlier had relayed a more optimistic view of the future from the Lord in these words:

"If a man is just
And does what is lawful and right; . . .
If he has walked in My statutes
And kept My judgments faithfully—
He is just;
He shall surely live!"
Says the Lord GOD (Ezekiel 18:5, 9, NKJV).

That prophecy is found in Ezekiel 18, a chapter that sets forth a fundamental principle of our human relationship to God. Chapter 18 looks at a question that was very important in the minds of the people living in Ezekiel's day: When tragedy came, was it because of what they had done, or because of what their ancestors had done?

Apparently a proverb had become popular in town that went something like this:

" 'The fathers have eaten sour grapes,
And the children's teeth are set on edge' " (verse 2, NKJV).

People were claiming that the disasters they were suffering were God's punishment for wrongs done generations earlier.

Ezekiel responded to that nonsense with a very plain message from God: *You're not being punished for what someone else did; you're being punished for your own sins.*

While that sort of candor may be hard to accept, there is a hopeful side to it. It holds out the hope that if people would repent, their circumstances would improve.

But by the time we come to Ezekiel chapter 21, written just a year later, we find a less hopeful message. And in it the Lord reveals that judgment is coming on everyone. No one will be spared its effects. "I will draw My sword out of its sheath and cut off both righteous and wicked from you," the Lord says (verse 3, NKJV).

ATTEMPTS TO GLOSS OVER THESE PASSAGES CAN IN THE END DO MORE HARM THAN GOOD.

How do we respond today to this very direct statement from the Lord, through His prophet, that He Himself will draw His sword and cut off both the righteous and the wicked?

It is popular in some schools of biblical interpretation to reinterpret the calamities that befell God's people and say that God simply *allowed* disaster to descend—He didn't take an active role in punishing the people.

While that sort of teaching may make us feel more comfortable in our relationship with God, it leaves unanswered questions about why God so often spoke through His prophets in terms like these, and why He instructed the man known as The Prophet (Moses) to warn His people of the severe punishments the Lord Himself would send upon them if they did not obey Him (see Deuteronomy 28:15–68 for example).

Through years of Bible study and talking with Bible students, I have come to believe that attempts to gloss over these passages, trying to soften the image of God and make Him more acceptable to modern sensibilities, can in the end do more harm than good. It can lead to confusion and a sense of betrayal and shock when those who have heard these explanations sit down and read the Bible carefully.

One of the chief reasons that we hear people give for abandoning their faith in God is that they cannot accept the harsh picture of God that their church has portrayed—for instance, a picture of a God who eternally torments people for not declaring their faith in Jesus. We go to great lengths to help people understand that the Bible does not teach eternal torment—and that is a good thing because it helps people see a truer picture of God.

But if we try to entirely gloss over the large sections of imagery in the Bible where God speaks of Himself being actively involved in temporal punishment of the rebellious, people who sit down and read these passages may come to feel that they have been duped by preachers who focused exclusively on the softer images of God in the Bible.

> I THINK WE NEED TO BE VERY HONEST IN OUR BIBLE STUDY AND NOT TRY TO MAKE EXCUSES FOR GOD.

I have come to believe that it is better to face these images head on and accept the fact that God often spoke harshly to the rebellious—in order to get a response—and that when a proper response was not forthcoming, God was true to His word and acted in accordance with what His prophets had spoken.

What I'm saying is, I think we need to be very honest in our Bible study and not try to make excuses for a God who speaks in terms we may feel uncomfortable with. We mustn't try to mold God into our image, or into an image that is warm and cuddly enough to meet all of our emotional longings. It seems to me that one of the reasons the Lord, in the Ten Commandments, forbade people from making graven images to represent Him was that He knew that once people's conception of Him was "set in stone," they would not listen if He spoke in ways that didn't fit their preconceived image of Him. We must free ourselves of the compulsion to create a God in our image, and instead leave Him free to re-create the image of God in us.

As we seek to understand God, we are left to struggle with some difficult questions. For instance, why would God, who had often promised blessings to the righteous, now proclaim that *all* are about to suffer equally, regardless of their response to Him?

> FORTUNATELY GOD SENT OTHER MESSAGES THROUGH EZEKIEL AS WELL.

We've all heard stories, haven't we, of a great tragedy—an earthquake or tornado—and how in the midst of great loss of life, one or two people were spared. And we wonder why. Were they somehow more righteous than the thousands around them who suffered?

And we wonder, *If I just do everything right—go to church daily, or at least weekly, say my prayers, pay my tithe, and help the homeless, doesn't that guarantee some sort of protection from God?*

We'd like to think that the world was organized on that principle. But the fact is that when evil comes, when tragedy strikes, the righteous and the wicked usually suffer together. In fact, Satan especially delights in attacking those who are closest to God. A tornado roaring through town seldom jumps over the churches and hits only the strip joints. When the airplanes struck the Twin Towers on September 11, 2001, those who had prayed for God's protection that morning, and whose lives were devoted to works of charity, died along with atheists and greedy stock traders.

And that's the kind of situation Ezekiel is describing. Only in this instance, it's not just some natural disaster like a tornado or a random act of violence that's going to strike everyone. This time it's a judgment from the Lord Himself—in the form of conquering armies coming from the north. (Remember Jeremiah's vision of a boiling pot in the north, spilling its contents over the land.) Armies will come from the north and destroy everything—good people's houses along with bad people's houses, the temple of the Lord, along with the houses of prostitution.

And the natural question in such circumstances is, What hope is there, then? If even the righteous won't be spared, why not just "eat, drink, and be merry, for tomorrow we die"?

If chapter 21 were the last chapter in Ezekiel, people might have an excuse for taking that attitude. But fortunately God sent other messages through Ezekiel as well. The Lord also gave him a vision of a better future.

Like this, for instance, from chapter 37:

> The hand of the LORD came upon me and brought me out in the Spirit of the LORD, and set me down in the midst of the valley; and it was full of bones. . . . And He said to me, "Son of man, can these bones live?"
>
> So I answered, "O Lord GOD, You know."
>
> Again He said to me, "Prophesy to these bones, and say to them, 'O dry bones, hear the word of the LORD! Thus says the Lord GOD to these bones: "Surely I will cause breath to enter into you, and you shall live" ' " (verses 1–5, NKJV).

In this amazing vision, Ezekiel is taken to just about the most depressing place on earth: a valley full

EZEKIEL IS TAKEN TO JUST ABOUT THE MOST DEPRESSING PLACE ON EARTH.

of bones—human bones, lying scattered around after a great slaughter. A still valley filled with the ghastly reminders of lost human lives.

In his day, a valley full of dried-up bones would indicate that something particularly terrible had taken place, for one of the worst curses you could put upon people was to tell them that when they died there would be no one to bury their bodies—that they'd be left for the dogs, birds, and wild animals to devour.

And that appears to be what has happened in the valley God shows to Ezekiel in vision.

So what Ezekiel sees is the aftermath of the fulfillment of the very thing he had been compelled to predict: the coming of an army that would destroy everything in its path, not even leaving enough people alive to bury the dead.

But as Ezekiel looks on, God has another message for him: "Prophesy to these bones," the Lord says.

And when Ezekiel obeys, things suddenly begin to happen. There are signs of life in the valley, as the Spirit of God begins to move among the bones. Ezekiel says,

> As I prophesied, there was a noise, and suddenly a rattling; and the bones came together, bone to bone. Indeed, as I looked, the sinews and the flesh came upon them, and the skin covered them over; but there was no breath in them.
>
> Also He said to me, "Prophesy to the breath, prophesy, son of man, and say to the breath, 'Thus says the Lord GOD: "Come from the four winds, O breath, and breathe on these slain, that they may live." ' " So I prophesied as He commanded me, and breath came into them, and they lived, and stood upon their feet, an exceedingly great army (verses 7–10, NKJV).

This is Ezekiel's vision of hope for the future. He sees the breath—the Spirit of God—coming upon his nation, and suddenly where there had been only death, there is life. The same God who promised a sword and destruction now promises life and resurrection.

IN THE MIDST OF THE DARK STORM CLOUDS THERE ARE RAYS OF BRIGHT SUNLIGHT!

And when this prophecy is fulfilled, it will fulfill another of Ezekiel's prophecies as well. In chapter 36, Ezekiel shares another encouraging message from the Lord, telling of how he will bring life where there has been only death. Speaking to His people who have suffered judgment, the Lord says,

> "Then I will sprinkle clean water on you, and you shall be clean; I will cleanse you from all your filthiness and from all your idols. I will give you a new heart and put a new spirit within you; I will take the heart of stone out of your flesh and give you a heart of flesh. I will put My Spirit within you and cause you to walk in My statutes, and you will keep My judgments and do them" (verses 25–27, NKJV).

Isn't that a beautiful picture of what God wants to do for us?

It gave hope to the very people whom Ezekiel had warned of disaster to come.

We see that over and over again in the Bible, don't we? While God's prophets are compelled to warn people of the results of their rebellion, they almost always relay a message of hope as well. In the midst of the dark storm clouds of impending doom there are rays of bright sunlight!

Ezekiel 36:26 is one of the brightest rays in all of the Old Testament, because in this precious verse God promises that He will return to His people, clean them up, reclaim them, give them new hearts, and place His Spirit within them to give them new life!

It's a beautiful image of what God wants to do for each and every one of us, each and every day of our lives.

If your spiritual experience has, by any chance, become dry, dusty, and in need of new life, God's promise is for you. If you'll come to Him, He'll pick you up, clean you up, breathe His Spirit into you, and give you a new heart that beats in rhythm with His own heart of love.

ENDNOTE

1. Jack Finegan, *Handbook of Biblical Chronology*, rev. ed. (Peabody, MA: Hendrickson, 1998), 256.

CHAPTER 9
_____

Daniel: Vision for the Future

Y ou've probably heard the story of Daniel and the lions' den. If you grew up going to church, you probably first heard it in kindergarten class. So I'm not going to retell that story as we study the book of Daniel. But if you haven't read Daniel 6 recently, take a moment to do so now. Because it is central to the book in more ways than one, I want to use it as the centerpiece of this study of Daniel's book.

The story comes right in the middle of the book, after all. But there's another reason I want to focus on it. In story form, it brings together the theme of the entire book of Daniel.

But let's look at the story from a different angle. Instead of just retelling the old story, let's try to picture what it was like from Daniel's perspective.

Try to form a mental image of Daniel on the day he was to be thrown into the lions' den. He's an old man by now, probably an octogenarian. As a young boy he had been carried away captive from Jerusalem to Babylon, and he's spent his long life in service to the government of Babylon, and later to the government of Persia.

IN STORY FORM, IT BRINGS TOGETHER THE THEME OF THE ENTIRE BOOK OF DANIEL.

But now, even in his eighties, he's probably still pretty spry. The story found in chapter 8 takes place just a few years earlier, and at that time he had traveled several days' journey from Babylon to Susa.

Picture him walking to the lions' den.

How do you see him? Is he walking confidently, striding right up

71

to the mouth of the den with his captors, sure that his God will deliver him from this trouble?

Or does he walk slowly, distractedly, prolonging the walk for as many minutes as possible—fearing that this may be his last day on earth?

At his age, you couldn't blame him for wondering if his time was finally up; whether he had lived a life of service to God and this was God's way of rewarding him with a quick end to the pains of old age.

> YOU COULDN'T BLAME HIM FOR WONDERING IF HIS TIME WAS FINALLY UP.

Or does he hurry toward the den, anxious to see the miracle that he knows the God of heaven will work for him? Does he expect one more amazing event in his life of wonder designed to convince his captors that the God he worships is the only true God?

If we remember the lessons of this story, we'll remember what the book of Daniel is all about, even if we can't give a detailed accounting of just what the king of the north or south did in which year, or even if we forget what nation is represented by the flying leopard in chapter 7.

So, what is the theme of Daniel? What is the lesson the book teaches over and over again, in almost every chapter?

It is introduced right at the beginning in chapter 1, verses 1 and 2, which inform us:

> In the third year of the reign of Jehoiakim king of Judah, Nebuchadnezzar king of Babylon came to Jerusalem and besieged it. And the Lord gave Jehoiakim king of Judah into his hand, with some of the articles of the house of God, which he carried into the land of Shinar to the house of his god; and he brought the articles into the treasure house of his god (NKJV).

In these verses, the introduction of the book of Daniel, we noticed two important points being made. First of all, the kingdom of Judah has suffered humiliation at the hands of the kingdom of Babylon. Items from the temple of the Lord in Jerusalem have been carried away and placed in the temple of Marduk in Babylon.

This apparently happened in 605 B.C., eight years before

Nebuchadnezzar's return visit to Jerusalem that climaxed in the peaceful opening of the city to the Babylonian invaders (the time when Ezekiel was carried away to Babylon). It was nearly twenty-six years later that the final, fateful siege of Babylon ended in the death of King Zedekiah and all of his family.

At first glance, the 605 B.C. subjugation of Jerusalem would make it appear that Marduk had triumphed over the Lord.

But throughout the book of Daniel, the curtain of the cosmos is drawn aside, and we are able to see what's going on behind the scenes in the councils of heaven.

The behind-the-scenes activity is revealed in these words: "The Lord *gave* Jehoiakim king of Judah into his hand."

Daniel lets us know, right from the start that the Lord hasn't been defeated. He's still in control. And in the story in chapter 5, He asserts that control when King Belshazzar begins to use "the articles of the house of God" as wine goblets at an orgy. Belshazzar literally sees the handwriting on the wall—courtesy of the Lord who has been anything but defeated.

That very night, final judgment fell upon Belshazzar and the entire kingdom of Babylon.

The same theme is repeated in story after story and in prophecy after prophecy: God is still in control. Those who exalt themselves and fail to acknowledge the Lord will eventually be brought low.

Daniel has seen that happen over and over again. And now he is facing punishment for the act of bowing and praying to the God of the universe. Don't you think he had every reason to expect that God would once again be exalted and His enemies humbled?

> COULD HE BE SURE THIS WALK TO THE LIONS' DEN WOULD TURN OUT WELL?

Still, though—could he be sure this walk to the lions' den would turn out well?

Picture yourself walking in his sandals, facing the greatest trial of your life. You've been snatched roughly from your prayer room at home—the one with the windows opening toward Jerusalem. You've been dragged before King Darius, the ruler of Babylon, and accused of a crime: praying to your God. Now, at day's end, after the king has tried everything he can think of to save your life, you're on your way to the lions' den.

You've heard about this place. Men younger than you, when thrown to the lions, have died of heart failure even before they hit the ground. Others have been shredded limb from limb before their feet could touch the floor.

As you get closer, you can hear the growls and deep roars echoing in the pit as the guards remove the stone that covers the opening. You know the lions are hungry, snarling at each other, jockeying for the best position to catch whatever doomed creature is about to be thrown in for supper.

Are you fearful?

Your mind runs back over your long life, reviewing other times when you thought all was lost and that your doom was sealed. You see yourself as a young schoolboy in Jerusalem, just finishing your studies, ready to go out and make a name for yourself as one of the nobility in Judah. But then the Babylonian army marches up to the gates and demands tribute and hostages that can be taken back to Babylon.

Suddenly all the good grades you strove so hard to achieve begin to conspire against you. Nebuchadnezzar is looking for "young men in whom there was no blemish, but good-looking, gifted in all wisdom, possessing knowledge and quick to understand, who had ability to serve in the king's palace" (Daniel 1:4, NKJV).

And unfortunately your good marks in school make you a prime candidate for deportation to Babylon. You can remember the day when a rough soldier looked you over, checked your school marks, and then said, "Congratulations! You're going to Babylon!"

You thought all was lost then—that God had abandoned you. But still you remained faithful to the Lord. When tempted with the fine foods of Babylon, you and three friends demurred, asking to be allowed to eat the plain food of your homeland, and God honored your faithfulness by blessing the four of you with the highest scores in your class.

> SUDDENLY ALL THE GOOD GRADES BEGIN TO CONSPIRE AGAINST YOU.

Then there was the time Arioch, the king's executioner, came to call—summoning you to the courtyard where all the wise men of the realm were to be killed. But in answer to your prayers, the Lord miraculously revealed a secret to you, and you were able to go to King Nebuchadnezzar and reveal both his dream and its interpretation. Your life was spared, and so were the lives of all the other wise men. So this isn't the first time your life has been threatened. You know the Lord is able to save you in times of danger.

And speaking of the interpretation of the dream—you learned something important yourself from that dream, didn't you? At the end of the dream, a stone cut out without hands rolled down and smashed a statue. As you explained to the king:

> "In the days of these kings the God of heaven will set up a kingdom which shall never be destroyed; and the kingdom shall not be left to other people; it shall break in pieces and consume all these kingdoms, and it shall stand forever. . . . The great God has made known to the king what will come to pass after this. The dream is certain, and its interpretation is sure" (Daniel 2:44, 45, NKJV).

In other words, the point of the dream was to teach the king that although he was powerful, God is more powerful and is able to countermand every order given by the king.

So, Daniel, are you worried about what will happen to you when they throw you into the lions' den?

You can remember what happened to your three friends on the day when everyone was supposed to bow down to the golden statue Nebuchadnezzar had set up. They refused to bow down to this god of the Babylonians, and, as a result, they were sentenced to death by burning in a brick kiln. When the king pleaded with them to bow rather than burn, they responded with these courageous words:

YOU DON'T KNOW WHETHER GOD HAS A MIRACLE IN STORE FOR YOU TODAY.

> "Our God whom we serve is able to deliver us from the burning fiery furnace, and He will deliver us from your hand, O king. *But if not,* let it be known to you, O king, that we do not serve your gods, nor will we worship the gold image which you have set up" (Daniel 3:17, 18, NKJV; emphasis added).

Remembering that day gives you courage, doesn't it? Those young fellows didn't know for sure that God would work a miracle to save them. But they still wouldn't bow to anyone but the Lord.

And you feel the same way. You don't know whether God has a miracle in store for you today, but you'll still continue to trust in Him. Because even if you die today, God has revealed to you that He has a good plan for your future.

There was that dream you had in the days of King Belshazzar, in which you saw wild animals charging about, devouring and destroying the earth. At the end of the dream, once again God and His people ruled the earth. You know that God has a good plan for your future, no matter what happens today, don't you, Daniel?

So how do you feel as they lead you to the mouth of the lions' den, as they bind you hand and foot, and toss you like a bag of barley into that dark hole? Fearful? Confident? Resigned to your fate?

And now let's apply this to our own lives by asking a few questions of ourselves: How do you feel today as you face the challenges that life throws your way? Maybe you aren't being thrown into a lions' den, but is there some other challenge that makes you feel that you're about to be thrown to the wild beasts?

How's your courage? Do you go at life with your head held high, trusting that no matter what comes your way today, God has a plan, and He'll work out that plan in your life? Do you face your lions' den today with the faith of Daniel? Or has life thrown you one too many hard knocks? Have you been knocked backward one too many times to face life with a defiant grin?

> GOD HAS A BETTER PLAN FOR THE FUTURE FOR THOSE WHO TRUST IN HIM.

If your courage is wavering a bit, go back and read that classic book in the Old Testament, the book of Daniel. Relish each of its stories, each of its visions, each of its prophecies once again, and focus on the fact that no matter how dire the circumstances, God always comes out the winner and delivers His people.

In almost every chapter, you see a situation go from bad to best instead of bad to worse. When Daniel is taken captive, he ends up teaching the Babylonian king about God's blessings. In vision after vision, he learns again and again that in the future, although armies will be allowed to tramp about the earth wreaking havoc for a time, each in its time will be reined in by God's great, overall plan. And ultimately God will set up a righteous kingdom where peace and grace will rule eternally.

However bad things get, God has a better plan for the future for those who trust in Him.

The book of Daniel is no Pollyanna story. It's a story about real people who saw God's hand working in their lives. It's also a book about the future and how God wants to work things out for the best for you and for me.

So, Daniel, how are you feeling as you face your lions' den today? Remember, Daniel's God had a plan for him and delivered him from the mouth of the lions. He spent that long, dark night sleeping with the cats, and in the morning he was delivered from his enemies.

How are you feeling today, friend? Do you face challenges with gaping maws like lions that threaten to take you apart piece by piece? Take courage. Remember the lesson of Daniel: even when it seems as though He has gone down in defeat, God is still in control.

I thank God for the book of Daniel. It gives me courage as I face each new challenge, each new den of lions that life sends my way. I hope it gives you courage too.

CHAPTER 10

Hosea: The Pleading Prophet

The book of Hosea is startling—even shocking in its frankness. It is full of emotion and pathos. Its raw power flows from the heart of a loving but spurned God.

Hosea gives voice to the pleading of a broken-hearted Deity. He doesn't speak in abstract terms. His words pour from his own wounded soul, pleading for Israel to return to their God. Hosea brings God to us on a very personal level.

Like so many prophets of his day, Hosea's life was turned upside down one day when he heard the voice of the Lord. God's message was impossible to ignore! "Hosea," God said, "Go, take to yourself an adulterous wife and children of unfaithfulness, because the land is guilty of the vilest adultery in departing from the LORD" (Hosea 1:2, NIV).

With his ministry jump-started in such a graphic way, Hosea could not be a detached messenger of the Lord, mouthing words that had not touched his own soul. God called him to *live* His message. To live out, on a human level, the experience of a God who had tenderly loved His people, His bride, only to have her spurn Him for the momentary pleasures of an adulterous relationship with other lovers.

Hosea experienced what God had experienced. And he spoke from a heart cut to the quick by a riven relationship.

HOSEA EXPERIENCED WHAT GOD HAD EXPERIENCED.

God Himself was suffering the pain of rejection, you see. His people, Israel—the people He had rescued from slavery in Egypt—had turned their backs on Him despite all the good He had done for them, despite all the love He had shown them.

Israel's relationship with God had been rocky from the start, and lately it had gotten a lot worse.

The name *Israel* in this story applies to the kingdom formed by the ten northern tribes that split off from the kingdom of Judah shortly after the death of King Solomon.

Both Israel and Judah continued to worship the Lord—technically—but in different ways and at different places. Israel's first independent king, Jeroboam, built two new temples, one in Bethel at the south end of his kingdom, and one in Dan at the north end. (This was Jeroboam I, not Jeroboam II, who is mentioned in the chapters on Jonah and Amos, and also figures in the story of Hosea.) Jeroboam I's intention seems to have been as much political as religious. He built these alternate shrines to keep his people from going to Jerusalem to worship in the temple that Solomon had built.

And in each temple Jeroboam placed a twenty-four-karat gold-plated statue of a bull. (Prophets such as Hosea denigrated the statues by calling them "calves," not bulls.)

It seems likely, based on archaeological discoveries, that Jeroboam never intended the bulls themselves to represent God. Israel's neighbors, the Canaanites, often pictured their gods standing on the back of bulls or another animals. So the king may have intended the bulls as mere pedestals or footstools for the Lord.

But it didn't take long for the people to start worshiping the bulls—or calves—themselves, just as they'd done at Mount Sinai with the statue Aaron had made.

From then on, things were rocky between the Lord and Israel. Many of the people began to worship Baal and other gods of their Canaanite neighbors. The Lord sent prophets such as Elijah and Elisha to call them back to faith in Him, but the people never turned fully back to the Lord.

If you read the account in the biblical books of 1 and 2 Kings, you'll notice some interesting things happening in the years leading up to Hosea's ministry. Kings such as Omri and Ahab seemed devoted to Baal worship, but at the same time they often listened to the Lord's prophets, taking their advice on how to conduct their wars.

Talk about pragmatic religion! Use the prophets for your political gain, but ignore their religious messages. Not that any politician today would go to church just to put on a religious façade! Not that anyone today would join a church just to increase their social or business network!

Well, back in the days of the biblical prophets, it appeared that this sort of hypocrisy actually paid off pretty well. Take Ahab, for example. He goes down in history as one of Israel's most wicked kings. Here's how 1 Kings describes his unfaithfulness to the Lord:

> Ahab son of Omri did more evil in the eyes of the LORD than any of those before him. He . . . married Jezebel daughter of Ethbaal king of the Sidonians, and began to serve Baal and worship him. He set up an altar for Baal in the temple of Baal that he built in Samaria (1 Kings 16:30–32, NIV).

But here's the thing most people don't realize. Ahab's unfaithfulness—his courting of Baal along with the Lord—*seemed* to pay big dividends. While playing both ends against the middle—listening to the Lord's military advice on the one hand, but worshiping Baal on the other—Ahab prospered greatly.

By marrying Jezebel, daughter of the Phoenician king of Sidon, he formed a trading alliance that brought immense wealth to his kingdom. Here's the testimony written about him at the end of his life: "As for the other events of Ahab's reign, including all he did, the palace he built and inlaid with ivory, and the cities he fortified, are they not written in the book of the annals of the kings of Israel?" (1 Kings 22:39, NIV).

> IT APPEARED THAT THIS SORT OF HYPOCRISY ACTUALLY PAID OFF PRETTY WELL.

Ahab built a splendid palace, with woodwork inlaid with imported ivory. He fortified cities and extended Israel's borders. In the year 853 B.C., when a dozen kings from northern Palestine formed a coalition that beat back an Assyrian army, Ahab contributed two-thousand war chariots to the effort, more than any other king.

Israel prospered politically under Ahab's leadership and continued to prosper under his son, Joram. But Joram was killed by a soldier named Jehu, who had been proclaimed king by a prophet of the Lord. Jehu quickly executed all the prophets of Baal and decreed that the people should worship the Lord only.

That was good news. But it didn't do much for Israel's political or economic prestige. A few years later, when Jehu's son was king, the country's borders had shrunk, and the army could muster only *ten* chariots!

Now, here's the question: If you were an Israelite living in those circumstances, is there any chance that you might be tempted to take the "pragmatic" view of religion?

Would you be tempted to say, "Things went a lot better for us when we were worshiping Baal"? Would you, just maybe, be among those who started going to the high places and offering sacrifices to Baal, in hopes that things would improve? (Later, as we noticed in the chapter on Jeremiah, people in Judah took the same prosperity-oriented view of the purpose of religion.)

Many Israelites did turn to other gods. And amazingly, when they abandoned the path of faithfulness to the Lord, their economic situation improved. Under Jehu's grandson Jehoash and great-grandson Jeroboam II, Israel started to prosper again—despite these kings' turning away from loyalty to the Lord.

Then, just as the recession seems to have given way to long-term growth, along comes Hosea with a message from the Lord that runs contrary to what the Wall Street gurus are saying.

He looks at the situation with God-given insight and sees that all of this prosperity, while good in the short term, will lead to disaster in the end, because the people have turned away from the Lord. And it's his divinely mandated mission to get this message across to the people, to convey a warning. But more than a warning. There was more to it than that.

God was not content to merely warn of dire consequences for apostasy. He had to put His heart into it. He had to plead—to appeal with all the emotion of a wounded lover for His bride to return.

Let's be perfectly clear about Hosea's circumstances. He's called to speak for God in a time of unparalleled prosperity in his country. Everything seems to be going well. And in many people's eyes, it's not a time of apostasy at all. They still worship the Lord—with enthusiasm and joy! They've built more altars for sacrifice than ever before. Hosea testifies that "Israel was a spreading vine; he brought forth fruit for himself. As his fruit

> WHEN THEY ABANDONED THE PATH OF FAITHFULNESS TO THE LORD, THEIR ECONOMIC SITUATION IMPROVED.

increased, he built more altars; as his land prospered, he adorned his sacred stones" (Hosea 10:1, NIV). The people see themselves as very devoted to God and, with seemingly good reason, based on empirical evidence, believe that it is their *dual* devotion to the Lord and Baal that has led to their prosperity.

But God doesn't see it that way. He's unwilling to play second fiddle to anyone. In fact, He's unwilling to play any instrument in an orchestra of gods. He alone is God, and He won't accept halfhearted worship. He must either be Israel's *only* God, or He won't be their God at all. Hear His message in Hosea 5:6: "When they go with their flocks and herds to seek the LORD, they will not find him; he has withdrawn himself from them" (NIV).

This is such an important message, especially for our day and age, right now, when religion is very popular in America—but mainly as a sort of interesting sideline—something we do once a week for a few hours. But still today the Lord wants to be your God. He wants to be the most important Being in your life *every* day. When we turn aside from Him or make other things more important, we're doing much the same thing that Israel was doing in Hosea's day.

It was Hosea's job to call Israel back to true and total devotion to the Lord. And he prosecuted his task with vigor! The Lord knew how to get people's attention, and He hoped that something in Hosea's mission would not only make people think—He hoped it would change them.

And so Hosea, this humble, clean-living servant of the Lord, went down to the red-light district one day. His very presence there must have raised a lot of eyebrows and started tongues wagging! When he headed home with one of the best-known prostitutes in tow, well, the gossip mill must have spun right out of its socket! If there had been tabloids in those days, the headlines would have blazoned "Preacher Weds Prostitute!"

Then Hosea and his prostitute wife started having babies and giving them provocative names. Hosea named son number one Jezreel, a name that proclaimed judgment for past sins. When a daughter came along, he named her "Not pitied," her very name proclaiming that God would no longer pity His people. Son number two was named "Not My people," a prophecy that God would no longer consider Israel His chosen nation.

> HE'S UNWILLING TO PLAY ANY INSTRUMENT IN AN ORCHESTRA OF GODS.

The next story to hit the gossip mill reported that after making three babies with him, Hosea's prostitute wife ran away and moved back in with her old pimp!

But even then, Hosea didn't give up on her—just as God had not given up on His people. God called him to demonstrate his love in just the way that God continued to demonstrate His love to Israel:

> The Lord said to me, "Go, show your love to your wife again, though she is loved by another and is an adulteress. Love her as the Lord loves the Israelites, though they turn to other gods. . . ."
> So I bought her for fifteen shekels of silver and about a homer and a lethek of barley (Hosea 3:1, 2, NIV).

What an amazing, practical demonstration of God's love for His wayward people!

I hope you'll take the time to read the fourteen-chapter book of Hosea. You'll find it to be a book full of pathos. You can almost see the tears of God running down the pages as He pleads with His people—sometimes erupting in anger drawn from deep within His jilted soul, sometimes promising the most wonderful blessings if they will return, sometimes picturing the joys He wants them to have.

> YOU CAN ALMOST SEE THE TEARS OF GOD RUNNING DOWN THE PAGES AS HE PLEADS WITH HIS PEOPLE.

In Hosea we read God's heart-warming *and* heart-wrenching appeals to His people. Appeals that are addressed as much to you and me as they were to Israel of old:

> "How can I give you up, Ephraim? How can I hand you over, Israel? . . . My heart is changed within me; all my compassion is aroused."
> "I will betroth you to me forever; I will betroth you in righteousness and justice, in love and compassion. I will betroth you in faithfulness, and you will acknowledge the Lord" (Hosea 11:8; 2:19, 20, NIV).

That's what God wants for you and me today. He wants to bless us. He wants to love us, and for us to love Him in return. But He won't play second fiddle, or even first chair, in our orchestra.

He asks us to turn away from all other things and to worship Him and Him alone.

CHAPTER 11

Joel: Joy in a Time of Sorrow

You know how it is. Whenever something bad happens—a disaster, a terrorist attack, a school shooting—you can count on someone to stand up and say, "This is a judgment from the Lord! Repent or something worse will come upon you!"

And that raises a question that I think we Christians need to take seriously: How should we respond to these doomsayers, these seriously self-righteous proclaimers of probity and judgment? Should we shout them down, criticize them for their lack of love, and inundate their Twitter accounts with 140-character proclamations of condemnation?

Before we leap to judgment on those passing judgment, there's something in the Bible we need to look at.

People who proclaim that tragedy is sometimes a judgment of the Lord can find a precedent in the Bible in books such as the one that records the words of the prophet Joel.

When something terrible happens, we all go looking for answers, don't we? We ask ourselves: What does it mean? Is it time for self-examination or even self-condemnation? Is it time to take stock and ask whether this is a judgment from God sent to call me up short and make me change course? Or should we just blame everything bad that happens on the devil?

> HOW SHOULD WE RESPOND TO THESE SERIOUSLY SELF-RIGHTEOUS PROCLAIMERS OF PROBITY AND JUDGMENT?

These days when a preacher has the audacity to suggest that bad things are happening because God is judging our nation, he or she is quickly shouted down. People don't want to hear that kind of thing. And they didn't in Joel's day either.

We call people who go around telling others that their suffering is a judgment from God "Job's comforters." And we criticize their self-righteousness, just like the Lord criticized Job's supposed friends.

The story of Job and his comforters pretty well puts to rest the idea that whenever something bad happens, it's our job to go and tell the people who are suffering to straighten up and fly right.

> WE MUSTN'T DISMISS TOO LIGHTLY THE IDEA THAT GOD SOMETIMES THROWS STUMBLING BLOCKS IN OUR PATH.

Jesus Himself faced that type of self-righteous attitude when the Pharisees brought a man born blind to Him and asked who sinned, the man or his parents, to cause him to be born blind. Jesus didn't buy into their question at all but told them that the blindness wasn't the result of anyone's sin. It wasn't God's judgment on anyone.

But does that mean that tragedy and trouble are never the result of a loving God putting obstacles in our path in order to slow us down in our headlong rush in the wrong direction? Many of the prophets, beginning with Moses, predicted that God Himself would send disasters as punishments designed to turn people back to the right path. (See, for example, Deuteronomy 28, where God uses both the carrot and the stick to prod His people to stay focused and go the right direction.)

Let's face it. Sin often has bad results. The very reason God gives us rules to live b y is to protect us from those bad results. Remember, after Jesus healed one sick man, He said to him, "See, you are well again. Stop sinning or something worse may happen to you" (John 5:14, NIV). That story in John 5 is just a few chapters before the story of the blind man, so we need to see that there is a balance here. Jesus wasn't teaching that bad things never result from sin.

Another Bible text cautions, "My son, do not regard lightly the discipline of the Lord, nor faint when you are reproved by Him; for those whom the Lord loves He disciplines, and He scourges every son whom He receives" (Hebrews 12:5, 6, NASB).

That text is, of course, found in the New Testament, so it's not true that the Old Testament God was a God of judgment, while the New

Testament God is a God of love, as some people assert.

Those examples show that we mustn't dismiss too lightly the idea that God sometimes throws stumbling blocks in our path to keep us from going the wrong way. Remember the story of Balaam and the donkey!

> HE DESCRIBED THE DESTRUCTION WROUGHT BY THE MARAUDING MANDIBLES ON LEAPING LEGS.

The prophet Joel was called to speak for the Lord when just such a thing had happened. A terrible plague of locusts had come, devouring everything in its path, and it was Joel's job to tell the people that the terrible situation they faced was the result of their turning away from the Lord.

Looking at the barren land all around him, Joel asked, "Has anything like this ever happened before?" He described the destruction wrought by the marauding mandibles on leaping legs:

> What the chewing locust left, the swarming locust has eaten; what the swarming locust left, the crawling locust has eaten; and what the crawling locust left, the consuming locust has eaten. . . .
>
> He has laid waste My vine, and ruined My fig tree; he has stripped it bare and thrown it away; its branches are made white (Joel 1:4, 7, NKJV).

In her book *On the Banks of Plum Creek,* Laura Ingalls Wilder describes what a locust plague looked like to a seven-year-old girl in Minnesota in the summer of 1872:

> A cloud was over the sun. It was not like any cloud they had ever seen before. It was a cloud of something like snowflakes, but they were larger than snowflakes, and thin and glittering. Light shone through each flickering particle. . . .
>
> Plunk! Something hit Laura's head and fell to the ground. She looked down and saw the largest grasshopper she had ever seen. Then huge brown grasshoppers were hitting the ground all around her, hitting her head and her face and her arms. . . .
>
> Laura tried to beat them off. Their claws clung to her skin and her dress. They looked at her with bulging eyes, turning their heads this way and that. . . . Grasshoppers covered the

ground, there was not one bare bit to step on. Laura had to step on grasshoppers and they smashed squirming and slimy under her feet. . . .

They were eating the willow tops. The willow's leaves were thin and bare twigs stuck out. Then whole branches were bare, and knobby with masses of grasshoppers. . . .

In the plum thickets only a few plum pits hung to the leafless branches. The nipping, clicking, gnawing sound of the grasshoppers' eating was still going on.[1]

Joel describes the locusts in his day like this: "They run like mighty men, they climb the wall like men of war; every one marches in formation, and they do not break ranks" (Joel 2:7, NKJV).

Laura Ingalls Wilder says that when the locusts started marching,

No grasshopper turned out of its way for anything.

They walked steadily over the house. They walked over the stable. They walked over [our milk cow] until Pa shut her in the stable. They walked into Plum Creek and drowned, and those behind kept on walking in and drowning until dead grasshoppers choked the creek and filled the water and live grasshoppers walked across on them.[2]

In a time when we're accustomed to getting our daily bread from a well-stocked supermarket, it's hard for us to imagine the kind of devastation people who depended on the sweat of their brows and the calluses on their hands for sustenance would experience in circumstances like that.

> IT'S HARD FOR US TO IMAGINE THE KIND OF DEVASTATION PEOPLE WOULD EXPERIENCE IN CIRCUMSTANCES LIKE THAT.

In those lean, hard years, a man who had spent his last ounce of strength plowing and planting could feel the very life draining from his emaciated frame with each rattle of the gnawing interlopers' jaws.

How should the people respond to such a scourge? Through Joel, God appealed to His people to respond properly to the plague. He called them to repentance:

Gird yourselves and lament, you priests; wail, you who minister before the altar; come, lie all night in sackcloth, you who minister to my God. . . . Consecrate a fast, call a sacred assembly; gather the elders and all the inhabitants of the land into the house of the LORD your God, and cry out to the LORD (Joel 1:13, 14, NKJV).

"Now, therefore," says the LORD, "Turn to Me with all your heart, with fasting, with weeping, and with mourning." So rend your heart, and not your garments; return to the LORD your God, for He is gracious and merciful, slow to anger, and of great kindness; and He relents from doing harm. Who knows if He will turn and relent, and leave a blessing behind Him—a grain offering and a drink offering for the LORD your God? (Joel 2:12–14, NKJV).

Joel makes it plain: when bad things happen, it's time to turn to the Lord. Take the time to reexamine your life and see whether it's on the right path. God is merciful, Joel reminds us. Who knows, maybe He'll leave a blessing instead of desolation like the locusts left.

When trials come, when tragedy strikes, we can look to the Lord for understanding and help through the time. But let's not forget that His hand is sometimes seen in tragedy. Not that we should point fingers at those who are suffering and accuse them of bringing it on themselves. No, Joel's counsel is more personal than that. He appeals to his people: In this time of famine, turn back to God—each of you individually. Appeal to Him. Come close to Him and receive His blessings—blessings that will be poured out in rich abundance. Use your time of trial as an opportunity. Don't treat it as a judgment from God, but do use it as a time to consider how you can walk more closely with Him.

LET'S NOT FORGET THAT HIS HAND IS SOMETIMES SEEN IN TRAGEDY.

When you do that, you can lay claim to the positive side of Joel's message. Because, you see, Joel didn't just point out people's sins and call them to repentance, he also shared messages of hope for the future of those who would respond to God:

The LORD will answer and say to His people, "Behold, I will send you grain and new wine and oil, and you will be satisfied by them; I will no longer make you a reproach among the nations." . . . The threshing floors shall be full of wheat, and the vats shall overflow with new wine and oil. "So I will restore to you the years that the swarming locust has eaten, the crawling locust, the consuming locust, and the chewing locust, my great army which I sent among you. You shall eat in plenty and be satisfied, and praise the name of the LORD your God, who has dealt wondrously with you; and My people shall never be put to shame" (verses 19, 24–27, NKJV).

MAYBE THAT CURVE IS THERE TO TURN YOU BACK TO HIM.

And at the end of chapter 2, we find the amazing prophecy that the apostle Peter quoted in his Day of Pentecost sermon. He said that the events of Pentecost were a fulfillment of Joel's prophecy:

"And it shall come to pass afterward
That I will pour out My Spirit on all flesh;
Your sons and your daughters shall prophesy,
Your old men shall dream dreams,
Your young men shall see visions.
And also on My menservants and on My maidservants
I will pour out My Spirit in those days" (verses 28, 29,
NKJV).

This promise was fulfilled on the Day of Pentecost, and God wants to fulfill it in His people's lives today as well! But notice that in Joel, God promises that this sort of thing will happen when the people take the time to seriously consider their lives and to turn fully to the Lord and give themselves completely to Him.

If your life has hit a rough patch, Joel's counsel would be to use this time as a time to draw closer to God. And God will draw closer to you and carry you through the hard times.

Joel reveals a God who cares about His people—cares enough to throw an obstacle in their way when they've gotten on the wrong path. But who also cares enough to send blessings when they turn back to

Him. Even in a time of sorrow, Joel points the people to a God of love who wants to bless them.

So, when life throws you a curve, don't blame God, but do take time to reconsider your walk with Him. Maybe there is a way you could be walking more closely with the Lord. Perhaps He has allowed some obstacle to come into your path in order to slow you down and encourage you to take time to look around and reexamine how you are living. Maybe that curve is there to turn you back to Him.

But also keep in mind the lesson of the book of Job. When you or others are suffering, it may not be because of some misstep. It may be the devil's way of trying to turn you away from your faithful walk with the Lord.

These two books, Job and Joel, offer different answers to the perennial question of why disasters strike. The Bible is a balanced book that helps us see behind the curtain of history and our current lives and learn about a God who cares very much about us and wants to bless us as we walk with Him.

And what about times when things are going well? Does that mean that we can rest assured that we are on the right path and experiencing God's blessings because of our goodness?

Before you jump to that sort of conclusion, go back and read the chapter on Hosea and turn ahead to the chapter on Amos. Even in prosperous times, we need to keep our walk with God close and personal.

Walk closely with Him. He wants to put blessings, not obstacles, in your way. Walk closely with Him today, and then in good times and bad, you can have confidence that God is with you and wants to bless you.

ENDNOTES

1. Laura Ingalls Wilder, *On the Banks of Plum Creek* (New York: Harper & Row, 1965), 194–204.

2. Ibid., 264, 265.

CHAPTER 12

Amos: A Plea for Justice

Do you think you would like to live next door to a prophet of the Lord? Wouldn't it be great to have a man or a woman just over the fence who had a direct line to God and could answer all your questions? Tim Allen, in the long-running TV sitcom *Home Improvement,* always seemed to be able to get sage advice from his backyard neighbor, Wilson Wilson. But what would it be like to have an actual prophet of the Lord next door?

PEOPLE DIDN'T THINK IT WAS MUCH FUN TO HAVE A PROPHET IN THE NEIGHBORHOOD.

Well, people in the time of the prophet Amos didn't think it was much fun to have a prophet in the neighborhood. In fact, Amaziah, the high priest at the temple at Bethel in Israel, reported Amos to King Jeroboam's secret service detail for prophesying that Jeroboam would die by the sword. And Amos 7:12, 13 reports,

> Then Amaziah said to Amos:
> "Go, you seer!
> Flee to the land of Judah.
> There eat bread,
> And there prophesy.
> But never again prophesy at Bethel,
> For it is the king's sanctuary,
> And it is the royal residence" (NKJV).

Neither Amaziah nor Jeroboam appreciated having Amos in their neighborhood because before he came along, people had thought everything was just fine in the kingdom of Israel.

Amos was faced with a peculiar problem. How do you communicate warnings about a dire future to people when everything seems to be going OK?

When we looked at the prophecies in the book of Joel, we were looking at a very different time in history—just after a terrible plague had struck Israel. There we found the prophet of the Lord appealing to his people to respond to disaster by turning back to God and repenting and pleading with God to bless them again.

Amos, on the other hand, was living in a time when things were just the opposite. Like Hosea, his job was to prophesy about coming judgments and disasters—but during one of the most prosperous times in Israel's history.

> HIS JOB WAS TO PROPHESY ABOUT COMING DISASTERS DURING ONE OF THE MOST PROSPEROUS TIMES IN HISTORY.

Despite the common conception that because everything was going so well, God must be blessing the nation, Amos crossed the border from Judah and began to issue stern messages of rebuke and calls for repentance.

Amos was a poor and humble man, a field worker. But God called him to stand before kings, priests, and princes, proclaiming a message from heaven. He was called to the prophetic office during the reign of King Jeroboam II, one of the most powerful and prosperous kings in all the history of Israel.

Amos was a citizen of the kingdom of Judah, which had its capital and its temple in Jerusalem, but the Lord gave him a message to deliver to the kingdom of Israel to the north. The two nations had recently been at war with each other, and Judah had suffered a humiliating defeat at the hands of Israel.

Israel's capital was in Samaria at this time, and its people worshiped at the two temples that their first king (Jeroboam I) had established—one in the north at Dan and the other in the south at Bethel, not far from the border with Judah.

Coming from Judah, whose spiritual center was on Mount Zion in Jerusalem, Amos began his mission quite abruptly. Here's the introduction to his first sermon: "The LORD roars from Zion, and utters His voice from Jerusalem; the pastures of the shepherds mourn, and the top of Carmel withers" (Amos 1:2, NKJV).

The image is powerful. Obviously the Lord is not pleased with some of the things that are going on in Israel. And He doesn't just quietly mutter something about "I wish you people would change your ways." No. Amos says that when the Lord speaks, He *roars* from Mount Zion. And the effect? The top of Mount Carmel withers. Check your map. Mount Carmel, in Israel, is seventy miles from Jerusalem—as the crow flies! And Mount Carmel typically gets considerably more rain than Mount Zion, so the image of green-topped Carmel withering is startling.

God says that when He roars from Mount Zion in Judah, the top of the highest mountain in Israel will wither. That is quite the opposite of what had happened when Judah declared war on Israel a few years earlier. The battle ended in an ignominious defeat for Judah. Judah literally withered before the armies of Israel.

But Amos's rebukes are not only for Israel. He immediately launches into a list of nations that have done wrong and are about to suffer judgment. All the rest of chapter 1 and the first verses of chapter 2 focus attention on nations such as Syria, Ammon, and Moab.

This focus on the sins of other nations is an almost unique feature of Amos. Most of the biblical prophets were concerned only with what was going on in Israel or Judah. But Amos, along with his contemporary Jonah, reveals that God is concerned with justice and righteousness in all the world, not just in His own land.

> AMOS REVEALS THAT GOD IS CONCERNED WITH JUSTICE AND RIGHTEOUSNESS IN ALL THE WORLD.

Amos's messages to these foreign nations set the stage for the message God had given him for Israel.

But before he gets to Israel, Amos has a brief message for his home country, Judah. Judgment is going to come on that nation as well "because they have rejected the law of the LORD, and have not kept his statutes" (Amos 2:4, NRSV).

The messages to the surrounding nations, plus the message to Judah, sum up in a nutshell the Lord's complaint against Israel: injustice rules the day, and the people ignore God's laws. But Amos adds one more thing when he addresses Israel. And I believe that it is this aspect of his message that especially challenges American Christians living in the twenty-first century. The message that is especially addressed to us—to me!

Amos, under the inspiration of the Holy Spirit, speaks boldly against the injustice done in the land, but that's not all that the Lord has him speak against. He takes it a step further, beginning in chapter 2, verse 8: "They lay themselves down beside every altar on garments taken in pledge; and in the house of their God they drink wine bought with fines they imposed" (NRSV).

Here we see the depth of the corruption that is eating away at their spiritual lives, the religion—yes, even the worship of God's people in Israel. They have absolutely no qualms about robbing the poor in order to enrich themselves, then going to the temple and praising God for blessing them—even using their ill-gotten gain in the worship service!

> THEY HAVE NO QUALMS ABOUT USING THEIR ILL-GOTTEN GAIN IN THE WORSHIP SERVICE.

When I was a church pastor in the state of Wisconsin, there was a federal prison just a few miles from one of my churches. I spent quite a bit of time visiting prisoners there and became well acquainted with the Roman Catholic priest who was the full-time chaplain. One day as the two of us stood watching the prisoners filing into the chapel for morning mass, Father Kelly confided that several of the men in his congregation were powerful Mafia figures. Men whose money had been made through drug running, confidence games, shakedowns, protection rackets, money laundering, even murder. These men, the chaplain said, were some of the most faithful members of his congregation, never missing a chance to come and worship the Lord! In fact, even when they weren't in prison, most of these men were faithful members of their local parishes.

Somehow, in their minds they were able to make a complete separation between what they did for a living and their spiritual lives. Somehow the Lord's call for righteous living floated right past them. They seemed to think that all they needed to do was go to church once or twice a week—that's all that religion consisted of for them. It didn't touch the depths of their lives—the way they lived from day to day.

And that's the very type of thing that was going on in Israel in Amos's day.

How little things have changed in the past three millennia! There was no lack of religion in Israel. There was no paucity of worshipers at the religious festivals. No! The people loved to go to the temple at Bethel and have great feasts to honor the Lord!

But they didn't honor Him in their day-to-day lives.

To these worshipers who feigned devotion to God at yearly festivals while doing injustice daily, Amos spoke clearly. His voice boomed from the stairway leading up to the temple at Bethel, delivering the message of the Lord:

> "I hate, I despise your religious feasts;
>   I cannot stand your assemblies.
> Even though you bring me burnt offerings and grain offerings,
>   I will not accept them.
> Though you bring choice fellowship offerings,
>   I will have no regard for them.
> Away with the noise of your songs!
>   I will not listen to the music of your harps.
> But let justice roll on like a river,
>   righteousness like a never-failing stream!" (Amos 5:21–24, NIV).

When I read these words of Amos, I can't help but wonder what Amos would do and say if he came to our modern world. Would he perhaps take his stand on the steps of one of the popular megachurches and focus his withering gaze on the people coming to celebrate a weekly festival to the Lord? Or perhaps in the foyer of a little country church where worship has become little more than a weekly social gathering?

> I CAN'T HELP BUT WONDER WHAT AMOS WOULD DO AND SAY IF HE CAME TO OUR MODERN WORLD.

It's easy to go to church every week. And there's nothing wrong with that. In fact, it's a very good thing. But Amos makes us ask: Is it enough? Is this all the Lord really wants from me? As I study this book, I see over and over again the appeal for justice. I'm reminded that I as a Christian should involve myself in seeing to it that right is done for the poor, the needy, the war torn. I'm reminded that going to church every week and singing the praises of the Lord is not enough.

Amos challenges me. I hope it challenges you too. To do more for the Lord. To involve yourself in defending the downtrodden, upholding the unfortunate, helping the homeless. To reexamine every aspect of your Christian walk. To ask of every activity: Is this doing justice?

Is this not only legal but the *right* thing to do?

I have to confess. I'm not sure I would have wanted to have Amos for a next-door neighbor. He had a hard message for his people. So hard, in fact, that King Jeroboam wanted to banish him from the land. But it's a message God's people needed to hear. And it's one we still need to hear today.

Are we listening?

Now I don't want to frighten you away from Amos so that you'll never want to read his prophecy. So let me end this chapter with a little bit of good news. Although the book of Amos consists largely of a message of condemnation—a heart cry against the injustice being done in his day—he doesn't end his prophecy that way. He doesn't just tell the people that judgment is going to fall on them and leave it at that. Oh, no. Our God doesn't speak these words to discourage us, but to cause us to look up, to expect better things.

The end of the book of Amos is full of promise because God wants His people to reform their lives. And when they do, He wants them to know that He has good things in store for them. He wants them to have faith that there is an even better day coming when the injustice, the sickness, the sadness, the troubles of this world will all be over.

> "Behold, the days are coming," says the LORD, "when the plowman shall overtake the reaper, and the treader of grapes him who sows seed; the mountains shall drip with sweet wine, and all the hills shall flow with it" (Amos 9:13, NKJV).

Amos's message is that the Lord is good. So good that He doesn't hesitate to tell us when we've gone astray. He doesn't hesitate to send prophets to rebuke us when we need it.

And He also wants us to know that He has good things in store for us when we turn to Him. He wants us to lead honest and righteous lives. But most of all, He wants us to be ready to live with Him eternally—in His kingdom where, to paraphrase Amos 5:24, "justice *will* roll on like a river, and righteousness like a never-failing stream!"

That day is coming, and coming sooner than you might expect, but the Lord will stand by His word. The prophecies recorded in the Bible have been fulfilled, and *will* be fulfilled, when Jesus comes again.

CHAPTER 13

Obadiah, Jonah, Nahum, Zephaniah: The Judgment Prophets

I n this chapter and the two that follow, I've chosen to deal with several Bible books at once—lumping prophets with similar missions and messages together—rather than dealing with them individually. Doing so will help us gain a broader perspective on the work of the various prophets whose words are preserved in the Bible, and will keep our study from becoming repetitive and potentially tedious.

It's not that these prophets were redundant; each had a particular mission to a specific time and place. Each of the prophets covered in this chapter—Obadiah, Jonah, Nahum, and Zephaniah—warned of coming judgments.

EACH OF THE PROPHETS WARNED OF COMING JUDGMENTS.

Obadiah's message was directed at the Edomites; Jonah's, at the Assyrians of Nineveh; Nahum also proclaimed judgment against the Assyrians, but many years later than Jonah. Zephaniah warned the people of Jerusalem of coming judgment if they did not repent.

Let's begin with Jonah, the prophet whose message is most familiar because we've all heard the story of Jonah and the giant fish.

Put yourself in Jonah's shoes—or sandals if you will—for just a moment. You already know the story of his adventures at sea, but do you know "the rest of the story"? I'm referring to the story found in 2 King 14:25:

[King Jeroboam] restored the territory of Israel from the entrance of Hamath to the Sea of the Arabah, according to the word of the LORD God of Israel, which He had spoken through His servant Jonah the son of Amittai, the prophet who was from Gath Hepher (NKJV).

This simple verse reveals something very important about Jonah. He had a successful ministry as a prophet of the Lord *before* his call to Nineveh.

Jonah lived not long after the great prophet Elisha. He was an approximate contemporary of Amos and Hosea. Jonah and Amos antedate Isaiah by a few years, and Hosea probably prophesied in the early years of Isaiah's ministry. These four prophets served the Lord 100–150 years prior to the time of Jeremiah, Ezekiel, and Daniel. Obadiah, Nahum, and Zephaniah, on the other hand, fit into the same approximate time frame as those three later prophets.

Remember the stories of Elijah and Elisha? These events happened just shortly before the story of Jonah. In those days, the kings of Israel often consulted with prophets as they prepared to go to war. The word of the Lord that came to Elisha often helped the king avoid being ambushed by the armies sent against him. It happened so many times, in fact, that the king of Aram finally got frustrated. He started to think there was a spy in his war cabinet—someone who heard his plans and told them to the king of Israel.

> HEATHEN WARLORDS BECAME AWARE OF HOW GOD WAS USING HIS PROPHET TO HELP HIS PEOPLE.

But when he called his officers together to inquire about this, they told him that the problem wasn't with his counselors; the problem was with Elisha: "Elisha, the prophet who is in Israel, tells the king of Israel the very words you speak in your bedroom," they said (2 Kings 6:12, NIV).

Even these heathen warlords became aware of how God was using His prophet to help His people.

And apparently the same sort of thing was going on with Jonah. But the stories of how he helped the king of Israel defeat his enemies aren't recorded in the Bible. We have only this one verse that says that King Jeroboam expanded the territory of Israel "according to the word of the Lord God of Israel, which He had spoken through His servant Jonah." This verse reveals something important about Jonah, allowing us to understand what may have been going through his mind when the Lord called him to deliver a different kind of message.

The address on the envelope of this new message wasn't Samaria, where the Israelite king lived. It was Nineveh, the capital of the powerful and notoriously cruel Assyrian Empire.

And the message wasn't friendly advice such as Jonah must have given to King Jeroboam. This time it's a message of judgment: "God has taken note of your wickedness, and He's going to destroy your city unless you repent!"

That's not an easy message to deliver, even in a friendly environment. Obadiah, author of the shortest book in the Bible, proclaimed an unfriendly message to Edom, but as far as we can tell, he did it from the safety of his home country.

> BEING A PROPHET CAN BE A DIFFICULT AND DANGEROUS CALLING.

You might better understand if you imagine that you're given a judgment message and told to deliver it to Adolf Hitler or perhaps to a drug lord in some remote region where gangs rule with an iron fist, torturing and killing their enemies at will.

It's easy to understand why Jonah turned tail and headed the opposite direction.

It's not easy being a prophet of judgment. Remember our study of Jeremiah and the trouble he got himself into by speaking for the Lord to people who didn't want to hear the word of the Lord.

Being a prophet can be a difficult and dangerous calling, yet our merciful God sometimes calls prophets to deliver warnings to people in hopes that they will repent and avoid the coming judgments.

Zephaniah is another prophet who had a hard message like this to deliver. His was addressed to the people of Jerusalem. Here's how his message begins:

> "I will utterly consume everything
> From the face of the land,"
> Says the Lord;
> "I will consume man and beast;
> I will consume the birds of the heavens,
> The fish of the sea,

And the stumbling blocks along with the wicked.
I will cut off man from the face of the land,"
Says the LORD.
"I will stretch out My hand against Judah,
And against all the inhabitants of Jerusalem.
I will cut off every trace of Baal from this place"
(Zephaniah 1:2–4, NKJV).

Those are pretty strong words for a prophet to deliver—especially as the opening salvo in his message from the Lord. But Zephaniah, looking around at the evil, idolatry, and injustice that had taken hold of God's people under a succession of faithless kings, knew that smooth words just would not do. Under the inspiration of the Holy Spirit, he spoke out and called a spade a spade!

But did it do any good?

And what about Jonah's message of impending judgment—did it do any good?

Ah, here's where a little understanding of Bible history comes in handy. Because the answer is Yes!

Zephaniah, you see, prophesied early in the reign of King Josiah in Jerusalem. At the age of eight, Josiah inherited a kingdom that had

> UNDER THE INSPIRATION OF THE HOLY SPIRIT, HE CALLED A SPADE A SPADE!

gone astray for many years under the leadership of his grandfather, Manasseh, and his father, Amon. But Josiah's young mind was receptive to the message of men like Zephaniah. Second Chronicles tells us that

> in the eighth year of his reign, while he was still young, [Josiah] began to seek the God of his father David; and in the twelfth year he began to purge Judah and Jerusalem of the high places, the wooden images, the carved images, and the molded images (2 Chronicles 34:3, NKJV),

literally fulfilling what Zephaniah had said needed to be done.

The message of Zephaniah, though it may seem rather harsh to our modern ears, served its purpose. And the message wasn't all condemnation and judgment. Far from it. At the end of his message the prophet looked forward to what would happen if the people repented and turned back to God:

> In that day it shall be said to Jerusalem: "Do not fear; Zion, let not your hands be weak. The LORD your God in your midst, the Mighty One, will save; He will *rejoice over you with gladness,* He will *quiet you with His love,* He will *rejoice over you with singing*" (Zephaniah 3:16, 17, NKJV; emphasis added).

What a contrast! This is what God wants to do for His people—if only they'll turn back to Him. And when King Josiah repented and turned the people to the Lord, blessings followed. His kingdom expanded, and the nation entered a time of prosperity.

HE'D RATHER BE UNEMPLOYED THAN DO WHAT HIS BOSS WAS ASKING HIM TO DO.

And what about Jonah?

Well, you remember the story, I'm sure.

Poor Jonah. He'd been a successful prophet for many years, giving good counsel—counsel that led to prosperity for the kingdom. But then God gave him another mission: take a judgment message to the wicked, cruel people of Assyria.

Jonah didn't like that assignment. In fact, he did everything he could to get out of it. Worse yet, he decided he'd rather be unemployed than do what his Boss, the Lord, was asking him to do. Jonah 1:3 says, "Jonah arose to flee to Tarshish from the presence of the LORD" (NKJV).

He was supposed to go to Iraq to deliver a stormy message, but he decided to head for the sunny beaches of southern Spain instead. Maybe he could escape from God there—or at least forget about that troublesome message there.

Jonah was about to learn that you can't get away from God that easily. Maybe he thought that God would leave him alone if he just got away from Israel. But soon after he got on the cruise ship, headed for the Riviera, things started to go wrong. A huge storm came up, and everyone on board started praying for deliverance—everyone except Jonah, that is. Jonah didn't want anything more to do with God, and he attempted to sleep right through the storm. But soon the heathen crew was demanding that he pray.

Did you catch that? Here he is, a prophet of the Lord, and he's not praying! Instead, the heathen crew is praying and trying to force him to pray!

It's a dangerous thing to turn your back on the Lord and begin to flee. The Lord had not distanced Himself from Jonah, but Jonah had built barriers between himself and the Lord.

Jonah recognized that the storm was God's way of stopping him from fleeing, but he decided he'd rather die than do God's will! So he had himself thrown overboard. He literally was driven to suicidal tendencies by the burden the Lord had laid upon him!

But notice what happened as soon as they threw Jonah overboard. The storm ceased. And that led the sailors to worship the Lord. Do you see what's happening here? Jonah became a witness for the Lord in spite of himself!

And then, of course, there was the matter of the fish that saved his life and returned him to dry land.

What a miracle!

And Jonah ended up going to Nineveh after all.

And the Ninevites responded to his message, repenting and averting the disaster that God had said would come upon them.

Here's something interesting from the history books: we know that about this time, the kingdom of Assyria was under grave threat from a powerful kingdom to their north.

And we also know that in 763 b.c. there was a solar eclipse—which was regarded by the ancients as a fearful omen. The eclipse was followed by a serious plague that greatly weakened the empire. It just may be that Jonah appeared on the scene at that very time, when the people would be most receptive to a warning message like his.

At any rate, we know that the whole city responded with repentance—even the king in his palace. According to Jonah 3:6, when Jonah's message reached the king of Nineveh, "He arose from his throne and laid aside his robe, covered

> IF ONLY GOD'S PEOPLE HAD BEEN AS RESPONSIVE.

himself with sackcloth and sat in ashes," and made a proclamation that everyone in the city should "turn from his evil way and from the violence that is in his hands" in hopes that the Lord would turn away from them and not destroy their city (verses 6, 8, NKJV).

And when that happened, God did relent. He didn't destroy the city, at least not at that time. Jonah's message of judgment made a tremendous difference for the people of Nineveh—because they accepted it and repented.

If only God's own people had been as responsive to the warning messages of Jeremiah, how different their history could have been!

But, back to Assyria: a century and a half later, the prophet Nahum had a similar message for Assyria. But this time there was no repentance. In fact, within just a few years of Nahum's message, Assyria declined from her moment of greatest glory to a has-been. Nineveh was sacked and destroyed in a violent orgy of vengeance by nations that had suffered much under Assyrian rule.

Three of the four books we are studying in this chapter contain some of the toughest reading in the entire Bible—the messages of prophets who had heavy, judgmental messages to deliver.

But I hope you've noticed something important about these heavy, hard-to-hear messages: Sometimes they made a difference. They changed things. Which tells me that sometimes we have to go through pain and judgment before things can get better.

Though their messages were difficult to hear, I'm thankful that men like Zephaniah and Nahum had the courage to speak up.

> THESE HEAVY, HARD-TO-HEAR MESSAGES CHANGED THINGS.

I'm also thankful that God worked a miracle to make it possible for Jonah, who lacked courage, to deliver his message.

Even the tough messages contain plenty of evidence of God's love. And even if we're going through tough times today, that doesn't mean God doesn't care. It may only mean that He's waiting for us to turn to Him in repentance as Josiah did, and as the people of Nineveh did. And when we do, He's promised to pour out blessings on us.

Just remember, whatever your situation today, whatever trial you may face, take courage in the words of Zephaniah: "The LORD your God in your midst, the Mighty One, will save; He will *rejoice over you with gladness,* He will *quiet you with His love,* He will *rejoice over you with singing*" (Zephaniah 3:17, NKJV; emphasis added).

CHAPTER 14

Micah and Habakkuk:
Prophets in Search of Justice

In our journey through the Bible so far, we have encountered several prophets who cried out against the injustice done in their land and warned of dire consequences coming upon the people because of their failure to respond to the Lord.

Micah and Habakkuk are two prophets for whom injustice was a major concern.

Habakkuk, an approximate contemporary of Jeremiah, takes up the cause of the downtrodden victims of injustice by questioning God.

Let's put this in historical perspective. Because Habakkuk's prophecy comes near the end of the prophetic era, he can look back on centuries of messages from men such as Elijah, Elisha, Hosea, Micah, and Isaiah

> GOD'S PROCLAMATIONS SEEM TO HAVE BEEN IDLE THREATS.

who had spoken out against injustice. And yet nothing seems to have changed. The powerful are still exploiting the weak, the widows and orphans are still being evicted from their homes and left to starve in the streets. God's proclamations that He is going to punish the wicked and reward the righteous seem to have been idle threats.

So Habakkuk calls God's sense of justice into question with these words, right at the beginning of his prophecy:

> O LORD, how long shall I cry,
> And You will not hear?

Even cry out to You, "Violence!"
And You will not save.
Why do You show me iniquity,
And cause me to see trouble?
For plundering and violence are before me;
There is strife, and contention arises.
Therefore the law is powerless,
And justice never goes forth.
For the wicked surround the righteous;
Therefore perverse judgment proceeds (Habakkuk 1:2–4, NKJV).

Habakkuk is literally complaining to God, almost accusing Him: "Why don't You do something about this? The law is powerless! You never enforce justice!"

HE ASKS A LEGITIMATE QUESTION: WHY ISN'T LIFE MORE FAIR?

He asks a legitimate question: Why isn't life more fair? Why don't all good people have peaceful, healthy, rich lives; and why do cruel or uncaring people so often triumph over those who are kinder, more devout, more caring, more honorable?

When Habakkuk questioned God's justice, the Lord's first response didn't satisfy him. God's response in chapter 1 is basically to tell Habakkuk that the wicked will indeed be punished by the armies of Babylon:

I am rousing the Chaldeans,
    that fierce and impetuous nation,
who march through the breadth of the earth
    to seize dwellings not their own.
Dread and fearsome are they;
    their justice and dignity proceed from themselves
    (verses 6, 7, NRSV).

Amazingly, God seems to be saying that because His people have not been able to establish justice for themselves, He will bring foreign armies upon them to enforce justice.

Not satisfied, Habakkuk continued to question God and implore Him to enforce justice:

Are you not from of old,
    O LORD my God, my Holy One? . . .
Your eyes are too pure to behold evil,
    and you cannot look on wrongdoing;
why do you look on the treacherous,
    and are silent when the wicked swallow
        those more righteous than they? (verses 12, 13, NRSV).

Then Habakkuk went on to say that he was going to stand on the ramparts of the city—one of the towers on the wall where watchmen could keep an eye on

> BECAUSE OF HIS PERSISTENCE HABAKKUK FINALLY RECEIVES A RESPONSE THAT SATISFIES HIM.

the horizon to warn of approaching enemies. But Habakkuk is going to go there and watch to see what the Lord is going to do about the injustice in the land.

I will stand at my watchpost,
    and station myself on the rampart;
I will keep watch to see what he will say to me,
    and what he will answer concerning my complaint
    (Habakkuk 2:1, NRSV).

And because of his persistence in asking God for answers, Habakkuk finally receives a response that satisfies him. In the face of Habakkuk's insistent questioning, God finally answers:

Then the LORD answered me and said:
"Write the vision
And make it plain on tablets,
That he may run who reads it.
For the vision is yet for an appointed time;
But at the end it will speak, and it will not lie.
Though it tarries, wait for it;
Because it will surely come,
It will not tarry.
Behold the proud,
His soul is not upright in him;

But the just shall live by his faith" (verses 2–4, NKJV).

God's answer to Habakkuk, essentially, is, The things I have predicted will happen. It may take time. It may seem as though the vision tarries. But it will come about. In the meantime, what are you to do? Live by faith. "The just shall live by his faith."

> BOTH MICAH AND HABAKKUK PLED WITH THE LORD TO DO WHAT WAS RIGHT.

You want justice done? Learn to live by faith in God. And that is the theme that the apostle Paul picks up in the New Testament. He takes this phrase and uses it to demonstrate that salvation—not only from injustice, but also from sin—is by faith alone.

Habakkuk's plea for justice follows a long line of prophets who proclaimed God's indignation at the injustice done in the land.

A hundred years earlier, Micah had answered the call of the Lord to speak for Him about the injustice done in his day. Speaking during the rule of wicked King Ahaz, Micah pointed to the abominable conditions brought about by corrupt rulers, prophets, and priests: "Its rulers give judgment for a bribe, its priests teach for a price, its prophets give oracles for money; yet they lean upon the LORD and say, 'Surely the LORD is with us! No harm shall come upon us' " (Micah 3:11, NRSV).

Micah stood up boldly and challenged the leaders: "Hear now, O heads of Jacob, and you rulers of the house of Israel: is it not for you to know justice? You who hate good and love evil" (verses 1, 2, NKJV).

Micah was a prophet sent by God to call His people away from their selfishness and sin and to point them to the right: "But as for me," he wrote, "I am filled with power, with the spirit of the LORD, and with justice and might, to declare to Jacob his transgression and to Israel his sin" (verses 8, NRSV).

Both Micah and Habakkuk pled with the Lord to do what was right in a time when the people were doing wrong.

Now when you think about it, the appeal for justice in such circumstances is a two-edged sword. Good and bad. Good for God. Bad for the unjust!

What criminal, after all, wants justice to be done against his crimes? The Lord revealed to Micah why bad things were happening to the people in his day: "Can I tolerate wicked scales and a bag of dishonest weights?" He asked (Micah 6:11, NRSV). And of course the answer is No! As Habakkuk put it, "[God's] eyes are too pure to behold evil, and [He] cannot look on wrongdoing" (Habakkuk 1:13, NRSV). Speaking through Micah, the Lord proclaims that it is because of the wickedness in the land that "I have begun to strike you down, making you desolate because of your sins" (Micah 6:13, NRSV).

Micah and Habakkuk both hoped for the Lord to do right and to establish justice in the land.

> GIFTS ARE NO SUBSTITUTE FOR DOING THE RIGHT THING.

One of my favorite texts from Micah is found in 6:8: "He has shown you, O man, what is good; and what does the LORD require of you but *to do justly,* to love mercy, and to walk humbly with your God?" (NKJV; emphasis added).

Like other prophets whom we've already looked at in our journey through the Bible, Micah contrasts the seeming religiosity of the people with how they lived their day-to-day lives. The text we just read about what God *really* wants follows hard on the heels of a description of the kind of religion the people had come to rely upon. The prophet asks the rhetorical question:

> With what shall I come before the LORD,
> And bow myself before the High God?
> Shall I come before Him with burnt offerings,
> With calves a year old?
> Will the LORD be pleased with thousands of rams,
> Or ten thousand rivers of oil?
> Shall I give my firstborn for my transgression,
> The fruit of my body for the sin of my soul? (verses 6, 7, NKJV).

He's asking, What does God really want from people? Does He want sacrifices and offerings? And it's in that context that he presents God's answer: Those gifts are no substitute for doing the right thing. God will not be bribed!

Sacrifice and offering are good things in that they acknowledge our sin and our dependence upon God. But the problem was that the very people bringing the offerings would leave the temple and engage in deceitful business practices. As Micah pointed out:

"Are there yet the treasures of wickedness
In the house of the wicked,
And the short measure that is an abomination?
Shall I count pure those with the wicked scales,
And with the bag of deceitful weights?
For her rich men are full of violence,
Her inhabitants have spoken lies,
And their tongue is deceitful in their mouth"
(verses 10–12, NKJV).

The sacrifices and offerings weren't purifying the people, because people were simply bringing them to assuage their consciences.

Micah's reaction is similar to that of his contemporary Isaiah. Micah prescribes learning to "do justly, to love mercy, and to walk humbly with . . . God." Isaiah calls on the people to

learn to do good;
seek justice,
    rescue the oppressed,
defend the orphan,
    plead for the widow (Isaiah 1:16, 17, NRSV).

Both prophets want the people to understand that if they want things to be right in their land, they need to turn back to God, to walk humbly with Him, to become merciful and kind as He is, and to do justly—to do what is right.

And both Micah and Habakkuk look forward to such a day: Micah's prediction, found in chapter 4, is familiar. He writes of a time when "they shall beat their swords into plowshares, and their spears into pruning hooks; nation shall not lift up sword against nation, neither shall they learn war any more. But everyone shall sit under his vine and under his fig tree, and no one shall make them afraid" (Micah 4:3, 4, NKJV), and Habakkuk looks forward to the time when "the earth will be filled with the knowledge of the glory of the LORD, as the waters cover the sea" (Habakkuk 2:14, NKJV).

PEOPLE WERE SIMPLY BRINGING THEM TO ASSUAGE THEIR CONSCIENCES.

These prophets in search of justice understand that as long as we human beings have anything to do with how things go on earth, there will be trouble, fighting, and injustice. And so they look forward to the time when God will rule.

This is the hope that the Bible holds out over and over again. There is a final court of appeal. There is hope for humanity. There is a better tomorrow coming. It is promised in one of my favorite texts from the Old Testament, found right at the end of Micah's prophecy.

> Who is a God like You, pardoning iniquity and passing over the transgression of the remnant of His heritage? He does not retain His anger forever, because He delights in mercy. He will again have compassion on us, and will subdue our iniquities. You will cast all our sins into the depths of the sea (Micah 7:18, 19, NKJV).

That's what we all really need, isn't it? For God to subdue our iniquities and drown our sins! This doesn't mean that in the meantime, as we wait for the establishment of His kingdom there is no need for us to engage in the fight against injustice. Isaiah, Jeremiah, Micah, Habakkuk, and a host of other prophets give us examples of people who stood up for the rights of the downtrodden.

WE MUST STAND UP FOR JUSTICE. BUT WE MUSN'T NEGLECT MERCY.

We must, along with the prophets, stand up for justice. But in so doing, we mustn't neglect mercy. Micah also reminds us that God "delights in mercy."

We may wish at times that the world was a perfectly just place, where people were rewarded immediately according to their works, good or bad.

But what chance would any of us have if God did not mingle mercy with justice? What would happen to us if we immediately received our just reward for every sin we ever committed? After all, "The wages of sin is death" (Romans 6:23, NKJV)! Which of us would want to collect our full wages the first time we sinned?

What we really want is justice, tempered with mercy. And that's what our great God gives us! It is His joy to "pardon our iniquity, to delight in mercy, to subdue our iniquities." And as for our sins, when we confess them, He'll cast them into the depths of the sea!

Praise God for that!

CHAPTER 15

Haggai and Zechariah: Bridge Builders for God

On Scotland's east coast lies a picturesque estuary with the poetic name the Firth of Forth. Scotland's capital city, Edinburgh, is on the south bank of the Firth. In 1890, work was completed on the 1.6-mile-long Forth Railway Bridge across the firth—one of the most amazing engineering feats of the nineteenth century. The two center spans are each nearly a third of a mile long, and there's an interesting story about how those spans were joined, completing the bridge.

Construction crews had been working for months, from the two sides, building toward each other, toward the spot at the very center where the two halves of the bridge would come together. Then they announced that on a certain day the span would be complete—the final bolts would be put in place, completing the bridge.

People came from all around to witness the great event, but soon it became obvious that something was wrong. The engineers couldn't get the two halves to come together. Try as they might, with cables, tug boats,

> THE ENGINEERS COULDN'T GET THE TWO HALVES TO COME TOGETHER.

and heavy equipment, they just couldn't close the gap between the two sides of the bridge. It was an embarrassing situation, to say the least. How had their calculations gone wrong? They figured and refigured, tugged, pulled, pushed, and prodded. But no amount of human ingenuity, machine energy, or determination could solve the problem.

I'll tell you in a bit how the day was redeemed and the bridge completed, but first a spiritual lesson.

(By the way, there's a text in one of the Bible books we're looking at in this chapter that might give you a clue as to how the problem was solved. It's Zechariah 4:6, which contains this familiar phrase: "Not by might nor by power, but . . .")

The dilemma of the engineers at the Firth of Forth has a fairly obvious spiritual application. Think back to the first story in the Bible. When Adam and Eve sinned in the Garden of Eden, a gap opened between them and God. They could no longer meet face-to-face with their Creator. It was then that God gave the first promise of a Messiah:

> "I will put enmity between you and the woman,
> And between your seed and her Seed;
> He shall bruise your head,
> And you shall bruise His heel" (Genesis 3:15, NKJV).

These words became the hope of all succeeding generations. Yes, Satan had opened a tragic gap between humankind and God, but there would come a day when that gap would be bridged. The Messiah would come, as the Seed of the woman, sent by God—God in the flesh—uniting humanity and divinity once again.

THESE WORDS BECAME THE HOPE OF ALL SUCCEEDING GENERATIONS.

People all through the generations hoped that they would live to see the day when the Messiah would come.

As part of the promise of the coming Redeemer, God instituted a system of sacrifices and rituals to remind people of His provision for the cleansing of their sins. Innocent lambs and other animals were sacrificed daily to drive home the message: *Sin causes death, but God has made a way for you to be forgiven.* He will provide a sinless One to die in your place.

In the days of Abraham, these sacrificial ceremonies were carried out at hilltop altars. In Moses' day, God gave instructions for building a tabernacle with an altar for sacrifice. And then in Solomon's day, for the first time, God allowed Israel's king to build Him a permanent temple made of stone and cedar. The sacrificial ceremonies pointing forward to the Messiah were carried on daily in that temple for four centuries.

Through good times and bad, Solomon's temple stood as a testimony to God and to His desire to cleanse His people of their sins and to bless them.

But, as we've noted in other chapters about the messages of prophets, the ceremonies and sacrifices at the temple soon came to be misunderstood and misapplied by the people. Their attitude toward these God-given rites of cleansing ran astray. They began to view them as the only thing that God wanted from them. So the prophets often had to remind them that God wanted things such as justice and mercy more than He wanted sacrifices.

Finally, because of the people's unwillingness to repent, God allowed the sacrifices and ceremonies to cease. Babylonian troops burned Solomon's temple to the ground in 586 B.C. As a result, the sacrifices and ceremonies God had given to His people as a reminder of His plan to bridge the gap between Him and them could no longer be carried out. There was a great danger that God's people would forget Him—and would forget that He wanted to be their Savior from sin.

The prophet Jeremiah had prophesied about this time: "This whole land shall be a desolation and an astonishment, and these nations shall serve the king of Babylon seventy years" (25:11, NKJV).

The prophet Daniel was so concerned about the state of affairs in his day, when the temple lay in ruins, that he prayed the beautiful prayer of confession and supplication found in Daniel 9. Daniel pleaded with the Lord for enlightenment about when and how His temple and His people could be restored so that the ceremonies for forgiveness of sins could be renewed.

GOD WANTED THINGS SUCH AS JUSTICE AND MERCY MORE THAN HE WANTED SACRIFICES.

And God sent a messenger, straight from heaven, to reveal His plan—to reveal that a decree would be given "to restore and to build Jerusalem," and that that decree, and that rebuilding, would be a crucial event leading up to, and pointing to, the time of the coming of the long-awaited Messiah.

Restoring and rebuilding Jerusalem! Those were exciting words. They guaranteed to Daniel that the temple and sacrificial system would be reinstated—sometime soon!

Finally, the time came when God's people were allowed to return to the Promised Land and begin to rebuild the temple. But they soon became discouraged with the work. For a long time, they never got beyond building an altar and laying a foundation. For fifteen years, the altar stood in an open field, a pile of rough-cut stones surrounded by heaps of rubble.

Rather than rebuilding the house of the Lord, the people concentrated their efforts on building their own houses.

The desolate altar left the world in danger of never having the bridge built that would carry the knowledge of the Lord over from the Old Testament era to the time of the coming of the Messiah, Jesus Christ.

What could be done? How could the two sides of the bridge be brought together?

Back to the story of the bridge over the Firth of Forth.

While the engineers huddled nearby, scratching their scalps and shaking their heads in shame, something happened that brought the two halves of the bridge together.

The clouds that had been covering the sun blew away, and the full power of earth's mighty star shone upon the steel girders. And as they warmed, they began to expand and move ever so slightly. Minute by minute, the two sides moved toward each other, until they met, matching perfectly, just as the architects had envisioned.

The gap was bridged, not by the power of man, but by an outside power shining in and getting things moving.

And that's exactly what happened in Jerusalem back in 520 B.C. as well.

When God saw that His people were in danger of not rebuilding the temple, not building the bridge that would carry knowledge of Him to the world in preparation for the Messiah's arrival, He sent some special power down to bring things together. It came in the form of messages delivered by two of the last prophets of the Old Testament: Haggai and Zechariah.

> THE GAP WAS BRIDGED, NOT BY THE POWER OF MAN, BUT BY AN OUTSIDE POWER.

Haggai was the first to begin delivering messages from the Lord. In the late summer of 520 B.C., precisely sixty-six years after the temple had been destroyed (remember, Jeremiah had prophesied seventy years of desolation), Haggai stood up to speak: "You people say it's not time to rebuild the house of the Lord," he said. "But you've rebuilt your own houses!"

Then he delivered a message direct from the Lord: "Thus says the LORD of hosts: 'Consider your ways! Go up to the mountains and bring wood and build the temple, that I may take pleasure in it and be glorified,' says the LORD" (Haggai 1:7, 8, NKJV).

That got things moving. Haggai 1:14 states the following:

> So the LORD stirred up the spirit of Zerubbabel the son of Shealtiel, governor of Judah, and the spirit of Joshua the son of Jehozadak, the high priest, and the spirit of all the remnant of the people; and they came and worked on the house of the LORD of hosts, their God (NKJV).

In response to Haggai's message, the people started over again, laying stones for the temple, erecting walls, preparing a house for God to dwell in. But the rebuilding was not without difficulties, and apparently the work nearly stopped again.

So the Lord raised up another prophet, Zechariah, to remind the people that their ancestors had suffered because of a lack of faithfulness, and to call them to return to faith so that God could bless them. He opened his prophecy with this message: "The LORD has been very angry with your fathers. Therefore say to them, 'Thus says the LORD of hosts: "Return to Me," says the LORD of hosts, "and I will return to you," says the LORD of hosts' " (Zechariah 1:2, 3, NKJV).

Then he went on to proclaim God's mercy and His beneficent plans for the future of Jerusalem:

> " 'Therefore thus says the LORD:
> "I am returning to Jerusalem with mercy;
> My house shall be built in it," says the LORD of hosts,
> "And a surveyor's line shall be stretched out over Jerusalem." '
> "Again proclaim, saying, 'Thus says the LORD of hosts:
> "My cities shall again spread out through prosperity;
> The LORD will again comfort Zion,
> And will again choose Jerusalem" ' " (verses 16, 17, NKJV).

Zechariah looked forward to a time of righteous rule in the Promised Land, with a crown on the head of Joshua the high priest—a time when fasting would be turned to feasting under the Lord's blessing.

This prophecy about the Lord's house being built was given early in 519 B.C. Ezra the scribe reports:

The elders of the Jews built, and they prospered through the prophesying of Haggai the prophet and Zechariah the son of Iddo. And they built and finished it, according to the commandment of the God of Israel, and according to the command of Cyrus, Darius, and Artaxerxes king of Persia. Now the temple was finished on the third day of the month of Adar, which was in the sixth year of the reign of King Darius. Then the children of Israel, the priests and the Levites and the rest of the descendants of the captivity, celebrated the dedication of this house of God with joy. And they offered sacrifices at the dedication of this house of God, one hundred bulls, two hundred rams, four hundred lambs, and as a sin offering for all Israel twelve male goats, according to the number of the tribes of Israel. They assigned the priests to their divisions and the Levites to their divisions, over the service of God in Jerusalem, as it is written in the Book of Moses (Ezra 6:14–18, NKJV).

> JUST FOUR YEARS AFTER ZECHARIAH BEGAN TO PROPHESY, SOME OF HIS WORDS WERE FULFILLED.

The third day of the month of Adar during the sixth year of King Darius can be pinpointed in our modern calendars as March 12, 515 B.C. Just four years after Zechariah began to prophesy, some of his words were fulfilled.

Zechariah's prophecies also include many things that foreshadowed the coming of the Messiah. Does this passage, for example, sound familiar?

> "Rejoice greatly, O daughter of Zion! Shout, O daughter of Jerusalem! Behold, your King is coming to you; He is just and having salvation, lowly and riding on a donkey, a colt, the foal of a donkey" (NKJV).

That prophecy, which was fulfilled at Jesus' triumphal entry to Jerusalem half a millennium later, is found in Zechariah 9:9.

And how about these prophecies pointing forward to the ministry of Jesus?

> "In that day a fountain shall be opened for the house of David

and for the inhabitants of Jerusalem, for sin and for uncleanness."

And in that day it shall be that living waters shall flow from Jerusalem, half of them toward the eastern sea and half of them toward the western sea; in both summer and winter it shall occur (Zechariah 13:1; 14:8, NKJV).

Remember, it was Jesus Himself who promised that anyone who came to Him would receive living water. And in John 7, we read Jesus' invitation spoken in Jerusalem: "If anyone thirsts, let him come to Me and drink. He who believes in Me, as the Scripture has said, out of his heart will flow rivers of living water" (John 7:37, 38, NKJV).

Jesus took the prophecies of the Messiah, given through Zechariah, and applied them to Himself. He stood up and proclaimed, I AM the One who was promised by the prophets of old. I AM the One who has come to bring to fulfillment all the sacrifices and ceremonies performed at the altar, tabernacle, and temple yea these many centuries. I AM the bridge, promised by God, to close the gap between humanity and divinity.

But if it hadn't been for faithful prophets such as Haggai and Zechariah, humanity might never have been prepared to understand the mission of Jesus. It was from the sacrificial services in the temple that the early Christians developed their understanding of what Jesus had done for them by giving His life on the cross.

Faithful men such as Haggai and Zechariah had an important role to play in preparing the world for the coming of the Messiah. They stood up against popular opinion and said, "It's time to do the Lord's work, not just ours. It's time to build the bridge of God."

IT WAS THROUGH THEIR MINISTRY THAT WE HAVE COME TO UNDERSTAND THE MINISTRY OF JESUS.

We have much to thank these men for. Because it was through their ministry, and through the ceremonies of the temple, that we have come to understand and appreciate the ministry of Jesus—the love and forgiveness of God as revealed in Jesus.

Thank God for men and women like them, who stand for what is right and proclaim the Word of God, encouraging people to do bold things for the Lord, just when it's needed most!

CHAPTER **16**

Malachi: Preparing for the Kingdom

I n our journey through the Bible, studying it book by book, we've come to the end of the Old Testament, to the book of Malachi— and to the questions that were bothering people in Malachi's day. It's in this prophetic book that we find God's final word to His Old Testament people.

By that I don't mean to imply that from the time of Malachi on, God simply turned His back on His people and didn't speak to them until the coming of John the Baptist more than four hundred years later. No, in the intervening years, there

> I DON'T MEAN TO IMPLY THAT GOD TURNED HIS BACK ON HIS PEOPLE.

were men and women who spoke up for God and led His people in standing up for truth.

But Malachi is the last of the Old Testament prophets whose book is accepted as biblical by all Christian churches. And so we ought to listen carefully to Malachi's message, a message that was to carry the people forward to the time of the coming of Christ the Messiah. The book ends with this powerful promise about the coming of the Christ:

> "Behold, I will send you Elijah the prophet before the com-
> ing of the great and dreadful day of the LORD. And he will
> turn the hearts of the fathers to the children, and the hearts
> of the children to their fathers" (Malachi 4:5, 6, NKJV).

This promise was fulfilled in the ministry of John the Baptist, who came as a forerunner of Jesus and preached about the coming kingdom of God, calling people to repentance, drawing them together, uniting families in looking forward to the ministry of Jesus.

When Jesus' disciples asked Him why Malachi had prophesied that Elijah must come before the Messiah, Jesus told them, "Elijah has come already, and they did not know him." And Matthew explains that "then the disciples understood that He spoke to them of John the Baptist" (Matthew 17:12, 13, NKJV).

So Malachi's prophecy looks forward, and carries us forward, to the New Testament. It's appropriate that it is the last book in the Old Testament. The prophet's message was designed to prepare the people to maintain their faith and their worship of God through four centuries of waiting, just as the book of Revelation at the end of the New Testament is intended to strengthen Christians' faith through the time of waiting for Jesus' second coming.

Think of it—four centuries! How long is that? One way to get a grasp of that time span is to ask ourselves, What was the world like four hundred years ago?

Well, the first permanent English settlement on the North American continent had just been established. In England, William Shakespeare had recently retired to his hometown of Stratford-upon-Avon. And in Italy, Galileo Galilei was just starting to get himself into trouble by writing about things he had observed through one of the world's first telescopes.

A lot can happen in four hundred years!

But Malachi's prophecy would have to sustain people in their expectation of the Messiah for *more* *than* four hundred years! He probably didn't realize it when he was writing his prophecy, but for centuries his message would be looked upon as God's final word to the Israelite people.

THE MESSAGE WAS DESIGNED TO PREPARE THE PEOPLE TO MAINTAIN THEIR FAITH THROUGH FOUR CENTURIES OF WAITING.

As so often happens with prophecies, Malachi's message came at a time of crisis—a crisis of faith—a time when many people were abandoning their faith in God.

When Malachi comes on the scene, God's people, the Jews, have been back in the Promised Land for a little over a century. You'll remember that in 586 B.C., the city of Jerusalem had been overthrown and completely destroyed by the Babylonians. For more about that, see the chapters on the books of Jeremiah, Lamentations, Ezekiel, and Daniel.

Fifty years later, in 536 B.C., a group came back to Jerusalem to begin rebuilding the temple. That's mentioned in the book of Ezra. But it wasn't until the time of Haggai and Zechariah—beginning in 520 B.C.—that the people really got behind the building project and finished construction. That was about a century before the time of Malachi.

Haggai and Zechariah had called the people to repentance and rededication to doing the work of God in rebuilding the temple, and had promised that when people put God's service first, things would change for the better.

And things had improved. But apparently not enough to satisfy the complainers. They were the ones who claimed that "it just isn't working out the way we thought it would!"

If you've ever heard the Smothers Brothers' comedy routine, you'll remember that famous line "Mom always liked you best!" Whenever things aren't going well for Tom, he can resort to that line, looking at his brother and claiming that all of his problems stem from the fact that Dick always got preferential treatment when they were growing up. If only poor little Tommy had gotten more parental love, affection, and affirmation, none of this would have happened to him!

GOD DOESN'T SEEM TO BE POURING OUT THE BLESSINGS THEY EXPECT.

Well, when you start reading Malachi, you get the impression that some people in Israel had been making that same sort of a complaint to God—saying that He was taking better care of Edom, the nation of Israel's brother Esau, than He was of them.

Through Malachi, the Lord responds to that complaint by taking the long view. He says, You know what? It may appear that way right now, but let me tell you what's going to happen in the future. Even though Edom may rebuild its cities and seem to be more prosperous than you are, it's not going to last. In the end there will be nothing left of it, but *if you'll just trust in Me*, I'll continue to bless you.

But that's the big *if*!

If you'll continue to trust in Me.

The people have been complaining that God doesn't seem to be pouring out the blessings they expect. In fact, it's gotten so bad that people are starting to ask what is the purpose of even worshiping God. Here are their very words, recorded in Malachi 3:13–15.

> "Your words have been harsh against Me," says the LORD, "Yet you say, 'What have we spoken against You?' You have said, 'It is useless to serve God; what profit is it that we have kept His ordinance, and that we have walked as mourners before the LORD of hosts? So now we call the proud blessed, for those who do wickedness are raised up; they even tempt God and go free' " (NKJV).

In other words, the people are looking around and saying, "You know what? Being a good Jew doesn't really help at all. Repenting of our sins and bringing offerings to the temple doesn't pay good dividends. In fact, the proud who don't humble themselves before the Lord are getting all the blessings. Those who sin openly don't get punished; in fact, they end up better off than the religious!"

Now, you might expect that the Lord would respond to these complaints with words like Jesus used in the New Testament: "Blessed are the poor . . . for theirs is the kingdom of heaven" (Matthew 5:3, NKJV).

But that's not the tack God takes in Malachi.

In fact, you could almost say that God responds to the people's accusations by going on the attack Himself. But He's not really attacking them. He does point out though that the problem actually doesn't lie in His court, but in theirs.

IN FACT, THE PROUD ARE GETTING THE BLESSINGS.

Speaking for God, Malachi responds to the people's complaints by pointing out five specific sins that are shutting off the flow of God's blessings to them.

When the people complain that worshiping the Lord hasn't improved their lot in life, God responds by asking just how faithful they've actually been in their worship. "You offer defiled food on My altar," He says (Malachi 1:7, NKJV). He asks them how their governor would respond if they brought sick animals to him as a gift—would he bless them? Then how can they expect God to bless them when they bring sick and blemished animals for sacrifices?

Malachi sets up a definite cause-and-effect relationship between the people's faithfulness and the Lord's blessings. Because they don't live out their faith, responding to God wholeheartedly with perfect offerings, God doesn't respond to them with blessing.

But that's not all. In chapter 2, the Lord takes issue with the unfaithful priests and with the people because they have begun to freely practice divorce instead of being faithful to their marriage covenants. The implication is if you aren't faithful to your covenants, why do you expect God to be faithful to His?

He makes it clear that if the people want to experience His richest blessings, they need to consider their lives and their devotion to Him. They need to clean up their acts. And in chapter 3, the Lord promises that He Himself will do the cleaning up: "He will sit as a refiner and a purifier of silver; He will purify the sons of Levi, and purge them as gold and silver, that they may offer to the LORD an offering in righteousness" (Malachi 3:3, NKJV).

He then reminds them that they have even gone so far as to steal from Him by failing to bring faithful tithes and offerings: "Will a man rob God? Yet you have robbed Me! But you say, 'In what way have we robbed You?' In tithes and offerings" (verse 8, NKJV).

But He doesn't leave it at that. He challenges them to be faithful and to see what the results are: " 'Bring all the tithes into the storehouse . . . and try Me now in this,' says the LORD of hosts, 'if I will not open for you the windows of heaven and pour out for you such blessing that there will not be room enough to receive it' " (verse 10, NKJV).

IF YOU WANT GOD TO BE FAITHFUL, YOU NEED TO BE FAITHFUL TO HIM!

Over and over again, Malachi challenges the people who have been complaining: if you want God to be faithful in blessing you, you need to be faithful to Him!

The nations around Israel thought of offerings and sacrifices as a way to buy God's favor. In fact, the Greek philosopher Plato, Malachi's contemporary, included this idea in the discussions carried out in his famous work *The Republic*. One of his main characters argues that the wealthy will be most blessed by the gods because they can bring offerings to buy the favor of the gods.

But that's not Malachi's point. No, the sacrifices, tithes, and offerings he calls for must be an expression of faith in God, not an attempt to buy His favor. "Try Me out," God says (not "Buy Me off!").

Because it is our genuine faith in Him that opens the channels—the windows of heaven, as Malachi expresses it—to receive the blessings the Lord wants to pour out on us.

Faith and faithfulness—the two need to go together.

At the end of this prophecy—at the very end of the Old Testament—God makes another promise to His people. He promises the coming of the Day of the Lord, but before that happens, Elijah will come. That's a way of saying that God won't bring final judgment upon the world without sending a final warning.

He will continue to call His people to faith in Him, and to faithfulness in their worship, right down to the end of time.

He is faithful with us.

And He calls us to be faithful to Him. That's His plan for blessing us and saving us in His eternal kingdom.

Malachi and the Old Testament ended with a promise, looking forward to the coming of the Messiah. It was a promise that people could cling to as they awaited the coming of the Promised One.

Revelation, the last book of the New Testament, also ends with a promise—one we can cling to as we await the second and final coming of the same Promised One!

Who Were the Prophets?

In the Bible, the term *prophet* is applied to people with a variety of roles. For instance, Abraham was called a prophet by one of his neighbors. Balaam, who wanted to curse Israel, is an interesting example of a prophet who uttered the Lord's words even though he wanted to say something else! Miriam was a prophetess, as was and Deborah, a judge and military leader of Israel. In David's time, priests and singers such as Asaph, Heman, and Jeduthun and their descendants who served in the temple were appointed to "prophesy with harps, stringed instruments, and cymbals" (1 Chronicles 25:1, NKJV). Even King Saul was regarded as a prophet because on one occasion he fell under the influence of a group of men who were prophesying with "a stringed instrument, a tambourine, a flute, and a harp" (see 1 Samuel 10:5, NKJV). Elisha was also known to prophesy to the accompaniment of music (2 Kings 3:14–19).

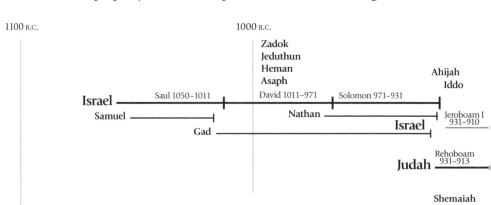

Names of prophets are in bold type. Kings and their years of rule are shown on the timeline.

Dates are based largely on the chronology found in *The Seventh-day Adventist Bible Commentary.*

More detailed charts by Ken Wade, covering all of biblical history, are available at vop.com or biblelights.com

Others included in the chart below include Gad and Nathan, who served kings as advisors, critics, and writers of history. Many unnamed men of God also had occasion to deliver messages at times.

Typically we think of the prophets as coming down on the opposite side of an issue from the position taken by those in authority: Elijah confronting Ahab and Jeremiah rebuking Jehoiakim come to mind. Kings often regarded the prophets as adversaries because of their criticisms and calls for repentance.

Prophets versus kings?

In reality the picture of the relationship between prophets and rulers is more complicated. Even wicked kings like Ahab often consulted prophets such as Elisha before going into battle, and there was a time when the king of Syria was so frustrated in his attempts to defeat Ahab that he thought there were spies in his camp. His advisors had to inform him that the problem wasn't with spies, but with Elisha who knew what he was going to do before he did it and warned Ahab (2 Kings 6:8–12). King Jeroboam II (793–753 B.C.) is also regarded as a wicked king, but his kingdom prospered under the counsel of the prophet Jonah (2 Kings 14:23–25).

Good prophets versus bad prophets

As you read through the books of prophets like Hosea, Micah, and Jeremiah, it's easy to find yourself wondering, *What was the matter with the people in those days? Didn't they know the prophets had a message*

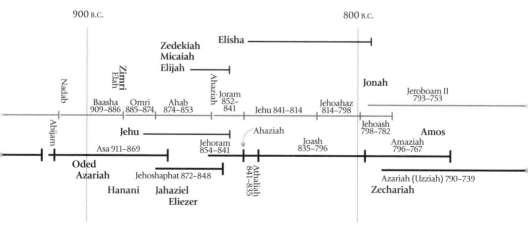

from the Lord—and that ignoring that message would lead to disaster? What part of "this is the Word or the Lord—fail to heed it at your own peril" did they not understand?

But the situation was not quite as cut-and-dried as it appears from our perspective with the benefit of hindsight. In fact, at any given time there was a multitude of prophets abroad in the land, and choosing which one to listen to might have been something akin to deciding whether to listen to a Republican or a Democratic pundit today.

Depending on who you listened to, you would get an entirely different perspective on current politics. I don't mean to trivialize the role of the Lord's prophets, but to their contemporaries, they may have seemed like just so many professional purveyors of personal opinions. And, with all due respect, the fact that even prophets whom hindsight reveals were truly delivering the Word of the Lord sometimes behaved oddly—walking around naked and acting out strange parables (see Isaiah 20:2, 3; Ezekiel 4:1–8; Micah 1:8)—might have made them seem more like troubled souls than trustworthy messengers.

Put yourself in the sandals of someone in Jerusalem in the days of Jeremiah. How would you have chosen whether to listen to Jeremiah, who prophesied certain defeat of your army at the hands of Babylon, or Hananiah and a host of other prophets who were proclaiming that Babylon's power would soon be broken (see Jeremiah 28)?

Or in the days of Ahab, would you have chosen to believe the words of the king's four hundred professional prophets (probably temple prophets—singers and musicians such as the ones appointed

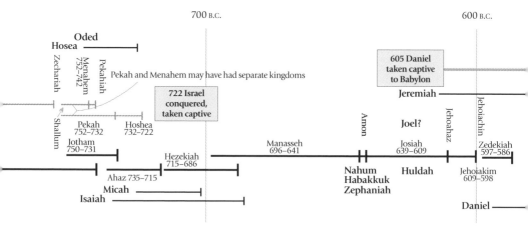

by David) who predicted victory, or the one lonely voice of Micaiah who spoke of doom?

It's just human nature to want to listen to those who prophesy good things rather than bad. And without the benefit of hindsight, you would probably find it difficult to know whose message to accept as genuine.

The end of prophecy

By the time of Nehemiah, we find that great leader and benefactor of God's people praying to the Lord to bring judgment down upon prophets such as Shemaiah and Noadiah who tried to frighten him and keep him from doing his work (Nehemiah 6:10–14). Seventy-four years earlier, Zechariah had prophesied of a coming time when the Lord would "cause the prophets and the unclean spirit to depart from the land," and when the parents of anyone who proclaimed himself a prophet would quickly kill him (Zechariah 13:3).

It seems that by that time in history, people had come to realize that proclaiming oneself a prophet didn't necessarily make one an authoritative messenger of the Lord. There had been too many deceitful prophets, and too many disasters had resulted from choosing to believe the wrong messenger.

In the ensuing centuries, the four hundred plus years from the time of Malachi until the arrival of John the Baptist on the scene, there, no doubt, were men and women who claimed to have the Word of the Lord. Some of them may have been genuine in their desire to hear and share God's message, but their counsels were not preserved for us in the Bible.

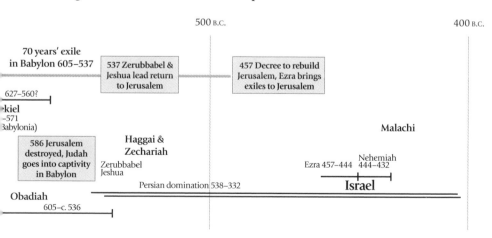

500 B.C.

400 B.C.

70 years' exile in Babylon 605–537

537 Zerubbabel & Jeshua lead return to Jerusalem

457 Decree to rebuild Jerusalem, Ezra brings exiles to Jerusalem

627–560?

·kiel
–571
3abylonia)

Malachi

586 Jerusalem destroyed, Judah goes into captivity in Babylon

Haggai & Zechariah

Zerubbabel
Jeshua

Ezra 457–444

Nehemiah
444–432

Persian domination 538–332

Israel

Obadiah
605–c. 536

Journey Through the Bible
From Genesis to Job *by Ken Wade*

For millenia, men have scratched their heads at the mysteries of God's Word. *Journey Through the Bible: From Genesis to Job* is a map to the Book of books. Like any good map, it provides an overview that will help you know what to look for as you search for God's guidance through His Word. Author Ken Wade will help you grasp the central message of each book and encourage you to persevere through the portions that may seem difficult or obscure. Any place you look in the Bible you will find a God that is full of love and grace for sinners.

Paperback, 160 Pages
ISBN 13: 978-0-8163-4309-6
ISBN 10: 0-8163-4309-8

Paul: A Spiritual Journey

With a blinding flash of light and a voice from heaven, Paul was transformed from a persecutor of Christians to an ambassador for Christ. Paul was changed in an instant, transformed over a lifetime; he planted the seeds that changed the world.

We are all on a journey. Through Paul's story and his words, the Power that transformed him can take hold of our hearts. In his life, we can see who God wants us to be, and we can catch a vision of the work He wants us to finish.

Paperback, 160 pages
ISBN 13: 978-0-8163-2493-4
ISBN 10: 0-8163-2493-X

Pacific Press®
Publishing Association
"Where the Word Is Life"

Three ways to order:

1	Local	Adventist Book Center®
2	Call	1-800-765-6955
3	Shop	AdventistBookCenter.com